What I've Learned
From My Daughter

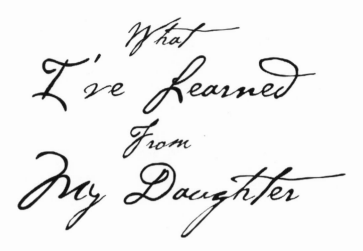

What I've Learned From My Daughter

BLESSINGS
FROM A SPECIAL CHILD

Nancy Jo Sullivan

Liguori/Triumph
LIGUORI, MISSOURI

Imprimi Potest: Richard Thibodeau, C.Ss.R.
Provincial, Denver Province; The Redemptorists

Published by Liguori/Triumph, an imprint of Liguori Publications
Liguori, Missouri
www.liguori.org

Library of Congress Cataloging-in-Publication Data

Sullivan, Nancy Jo, 1956–
    What I've learned from my daughter : blessings from a special child / Nancy Jo Sullivan.
        p. cm.
    ISBN 0-7648-1150-9
    1. Sullivan, Nancy Jo, 1956– 2. Parents of children with disabilities—United States—Biography. 3. Catholics—United States—Biography. I. Title.

BX4705.S878A3 2004
282'.092—dc22
[B]   2003069519

Scripture quotations are taken from the *New Revised Standard Version Bible*, © 1989 by the Division of Christian Education of the National Council of the Churches of Christ in the U.S.A. Used by permission. All rights reserved.

Portions of Chapter One were adapted from *Guidepost* article "Homeroom Lesson," © 1997. Portions of Chapter Three were adapted from *Guidepost* article "In the Waiting Room," © 1997. Portions of Chapter Ten were adapted from *Guidepost* article "A Rare Bond," cover story, February 1998. Reprinted with permission of *Guidepost* magazine, 16 E. 34th St., New York, NY 10016. All rights reserved.

Portions of Chapter Three were adapted from the short story "Date Cookies." First printing appeared in *My Sister, My Friend*, a gift book authored by Nancy Jo Sullivan. Portions of Chapter Seven were adapted from a short story originally titled "Twirls of an Angel." First printing appeared in *Did You Get What You Prayed For?* a collection of inspirational stories authored by Nancy Jo Sullivan and Jane Kise. Published by Multnomah Press; www.multnomahbooks.com.

Printed in the United States of America
08 07 06 05 04   5 4 3 2 1
First edition

To the Sullivan Clan–
past, present, and future

Contents

Acknowledgments

I wish to thank the following people: To John Cleary and Cecelia Portlock, my editors. Thanks for making this story shine. It's been an honor to work with you, too!

To Liguori associates; Bob Byrns, Sister Mary Margaret Doorley, and Father Harry Grile. It was a pleasure meeting you last summer. Our shared lunch on the twenty-second floor of the Raddisson was delightful. I enjoyed myself so much that I almost forgot about my fear of heights.

To Wendy Barnes. Once again you came through with an incredible cover. Praise you!

To Joanne Mason. You know the lessons of this book as well as I do. Thank you for mentoring me through the early years of motherhood.

To Maggie, an incredible therapist and friend. Eighteen years ago, you taught Sarah how to walk and talk and sing. Though I haven't seen you in over a decade, I still treasure the gifts you gave to our family; gifts of faith, hope, and love.

To Connie Petterson at North Country Transcription. I love telling people that you are my "secretary." It makes me sound so professional. Thanks for all your hard work. You brought this manuscript to life.

To Doctor Stephen McCue. Ever since Sarah's birth, you

have been a reservoir of support and encouragement. Your friendship is cherished.

To Marion. Throughout the years, you have been a shimmering star, guiding me on my journey of faith.

To Mom, my editor in chief.

To my precious family. Your names are written on my heart.

ONE

God Has a Plan

When I was growing up, I never thought I was very smart. In kindergarten, I was the last to tie my shoes. In elementary school, I was always in special science and math groups. It took me months to learn how to multiply and divide. The teachers told my parents: "Nancy can learn …she just has a tough time retaining information."

Now, I'm sure that the educational experts of today would have a definitive diagnosis for me—probably something like ADD (Attention Deficit Disorder)—but back then my teachers just scribbled notes in red pencil on my report card that read: "Nancy has trouble focusing."

Despite my academic challenges, my imagination was unstoppable. As a kid, I spent countless summer afternoons underneath an apple tree in our backyard, a spiral notebook on my lap, and a pen in my hand. I wrote hundreds of make-believe stories. Though my stories were poorly structured, riddled with misspellings, I dreamed of becoming a teacher and writing a book, not one or the other, but both. Often I prayed, "God…I know I'm not very smart, but someday I'd like to go to college."

I persevered through high school, struggling in the sciences, but passionate about the arts. I was drawn to the classic writers and poets. Each afternoon, as I read Shakespeare in the school library I would pray, "Lord, I'd like to learn to write like this."

I went on to college, majoring in English and supporting my degree with courses in education and theology. After graduation, I took a job as a teacher and campus minister at an all-girl's Catholic high school in St. Paul, Minnesota. During my first year as a teacher, I over-prepared for my classes. I didn't want my students to know how insecure I felt. Day after day, I would hear an inner voice say, "You're not smart enough to be a teacher."

As a young instructor, I would learn that true intelligence is relative. Life's most important lessons must be learned in the classroom of the heart.

The hospital room was wrapped in early morning darkness as flakes of November snow fell outside the window near my bed. My husband slept soundly on a cot next to me, but I drifted in and out of restless sleep.

I kept replaying events from the night before: labor... pain...a baby...a diagnosis...

I remembered clearly the doctor's midnight words, "I'm sorry...preliminary findings indicate that your baby has the symptoms of Down syndrome."

The digital clock by the bedside read 7:02 A.M. I was exhausted. I wanted to sleep, but unanswered questions kept me from rest. What did the future hold? How would we adjust? What would we tell our families?

Then I heard a knock at the door. I saw the silhouette of a young ponytailed girl in a pleated skirt, her outline shadowed by the dim lights of the hospital hallway. As she moved closer, I rubbed the tiredness from my eyes to make out her face. It was Jessie. We smiled simultaneously.

As she sat down in a chair next to my bed, I called to mind memories from a September morning just the year before. It was the first day of my teaching career....

I'd been assigned to Room 202, in a Catholic high school. As the school bell sounded through the aging brick corridors, twenty-one sophomores entered my 8:00 A.M. homeroom, a fifteen-minute block of time that preceded classes, a time reserved for announcements and bureaucratic tasks.

The students were all girls, all uniformed in the black woolen pleats and white starched collars of an eighty-year tradition. Carrying backpacks weighted with college prep books, they squeaked to their desks in polished saddled shoes.

"I'm Ms. Sullivan," I announced, as I wrote my name on the blackboard.

Jessie, along with the other girls in the class, watched closely and whispered. I too was uniformed, but I knew that my navy-blue tweeds and professional pumps could not conceal my youth and inexperience.

The mornings passed and those homeroom whispers found a voice in the brief conversations I began to exchange with my students. Sometimes we talked about academic pressures. The girls were worried about getting good grades for college. Other times the topics were more lighthearted— especially on Monday mornings when the girls bantered about the weekend, basketball games and slumber parties, dances and dresses and dates.

But somehow, it always seemed that the homeroom conversations flowed into curious questions about my life:

What had my first date been like?

Was the college I attended a good one?

How did I meet my husband?

They were like younger sisters eager for advice and insight. And though my college professors had warned against becoming too "friendly" with the students, I was honored to share what little I knew.

The year passed quickly. Then one spring morning in May, I came to homeroom clutching a picture of the ultrasound I had gotten just a day earlier.

Revealing that I was pregnant, the girls cheered and teased me about maternity clothes and support hose. "It will be a girl…for sure!" my students agreed.

Then, as I uncreased the black-and-white ultrasound picture that outlined my baby's heart and head and hands, they gathered around my desk—all except Jessie. She stood back from the group, her ponytailed blonde hair framing a somber half smile and blue eyes that hinted at sadness.

Homeroom ended at the sound of the bell. Most of the girls rushed off to their first classes, but Jessie lingered behind.

"Ms. Sullivan…can I talk to you?" she asked, her voice low, almost a whisper.

"Sure," I said, as I glanced at my teaching schedule. I was free until nine o'clock. We sat down in desks that faced each other.

"I'm pregnant, too," she said, her eyes now welling up with tears. "I'm almost four months along…I don't know what to do. My mom is divorced. She's worked hard to afford my tuition. How am I going to tell her? What will she say? What will she do if I can't stay in school?" For a moment, Jessie just covered her face with her hands.

"It's okay, Jessie...tell me more," I said.

When she gained her composure, she talked about the baby's father, a football player from a nearby school.

"He's been nominated for an athletic scholarship. We both know we're too young to get married...to take care of a baby. I'm so scared," Jessie said.

My glance turned toward a framed painting that hung next to the blackboard; a painted image of Mary, the mother of God, with her face haloed with light. Mary was a young unwed mother, too. Surely she must have felt fearful about all that lay ahead.

I wasn't sure if Jesse would receive the words I felt compelled to say, but I offered them nonetheless, "God has a plan for your baby," I said. "Don't ever forget that, Jessie."

As the last days of school approached, Jessie and I met often to talk. During that time, Jessie told her mom about the pregnancy. Jessie's mom responded with unconditional love and compassion, and began accompanying her daughter to birthing classes.

"My mom is going to coach me through labor," Jessie told me one morning after homeroom. I gave Jessie a "high-five."

During the final days of school, I met with the principal to strategize how we, as a school, might help Jessie and her family during the months of pregnancy. Much to my surprise, the school invited her to return to classes in the fall, even though her due date was mid October, just six weeks before mine.

All through the summer months, I thought of Jessie as I gathered gifts at baby showers and when I shopped for car seats, crib sheets, and bumper pads. Every time I felt the motions and movements of my baby, I couldn't help but visualize her meeting with social workers and signing adoption papers and paging through biographies of prospective parents.

Her plans and preparations for birth were so much different than mine.

When the autumn days of early September arrived, Jessie greeted me in the doorway of Room 202. Wearing a plaid maternity top, blue jeans, and tennis shoes, Jessie waved her class schedule at me. "I'm in your homeroom again, Ms. Sullivan!"

We tried to hug each other, but found it impossible. Our stomachs were the same size—enormous! We laughed.

Four weeks later, Jessie delivered a healthy baby girl. After a few days of recovery, she was back in homeroom, neatly uniformed. She showed me pictures of the baby she had given away, the daughter she had cradled in the hospital for a few short hours.

"I told her that I loved her, Ms. Sullivan."

Now, a month later, as the November snow fell outside my hospital room, Jessie had come to visit me. Though it was early in the morning, she wanted to be the first one to welcome my child. She had come to offer me the words I had once spoken to her: "God has a plan for your baby, Ms. Sullivan. Don't ever forget that," Jessie said, as she sat down on a chair next to my bed.

Our eyes met. For so many months, I felt compelled to teach her to trust in God's plan. How well she had learned that lesson. She knew it by heart. Now, trust was the tender lesson she could teach me.

Six years later, on a sunny, spring morning, I found myself waiting in my car at a corner stoplight; my window rolled down. Much to my surprise, Jessie pulled up right next to me in a small car. I waved. She honked.

There was a baby sleeping in a car seat right next to her. When the light changed, Jessie drove away, but my Down syndrome daughter and her two younger sisters called out in unison from the back seat, "Mommy, who was that?"

I looked at my three children in the rearview mirror. They were sitting side by side in car seats, with Sarah in the middle.

"That was a teacher I once knew," I said. "One of the best."

Ponderings

trust: from stem of true, a reliance or resting of the mind on the integrity, veracity, justice, friendship of another person; a firm reliance on promises; belief; hope. (New Webster Encyclopedic Dictionary of the English Language.)

Trust is a lesson that can only be learned in times of uncertainty. Having a child who is disabled, accepting a terminal illness, dealing with an unexpected divorce, a financial catastrophe, or a wayward child; all these experiences teach us to rely on God's faithfulness and to trust in his infallible, unbreakable promises.

In Proverbs 3:5–6 we read: "Trust in the LORD with all your heart, / and do not rely on your own insight. In all your ways acknowledge him, / and he will make straight your paths."

Though we may not always understand why God allows hardship and heartache in our lives, we can be certain that God is always directing our path. The Lord never abandons his children, even when unforeseen adversity challenges our faith. Sarah's birth brought much uncertainty, but it also affirmed God's unfailing presence.

Today, whatever you are going through, trust in the Lord. The "path" of your life is paved with the Lord's love. And God has a wonderful plan.

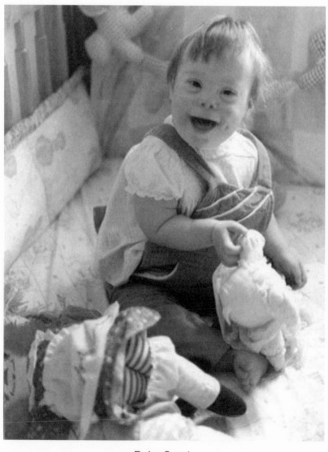

Baby Sarah

TWO

Feel What You Feel

I grew up in a large Irish Catholic family. There were eleven of us in all—my parents, myself, five sisters and three brothers. My father was a big man, broad-shouldered and thick at the middle. He stood about six foot four, a handsome, strong-jawed man who smoked Camel cigarettes, puffing them smoothly, with the mystique of Humphrey Bogart. A graduate of Notre Dame and a former naval officer, Dad ran a tight ship in our family—daily scrutiny of our rooms, weekly job charts, rations on cookies.

Every Saturday evening in our basement "rec" room, Dad made us polish our shoes for Sunday morning Mass. One Saturday night, when I was about twelve, I began showing my six-year-old sister, Annie, how to hold a shoe brush. She angrily whisked the brush over her small shoes as my brothers opened cans of Cordovan polish and my sisters buffed their patent leather flats.

"I hate shining shoes," Annie whispered as my Dad walked past.

"You've got to use more elbow grease," Dad told Annie. He held her small shoe up to his eyes. He made sure that he could see his reflection in the buckle. Seconds later, when Dad wasn't looking, Annie stuck her tongue out at him.

When we were very young, Annie was the only one who challenged my father. All that changed, a few years later, on a sultry Fourth of July.

On that ninety-eight-degree afternoon, Dad organized what he called the SULLIVAN OLYMPIAD, a series of backyard games that were mandatory for all family members. He had planned potato sack races, Lawn Jart competitions, and water balloon toss.

That summer, I was in my teens, and so were most of my brothers and sisters. We were growing up. No one was excited about playing games in the backyard.

Our sun-baked lawn was dotted with American flags and orange construction cones that Dad had set up to mark each event. My father stood on our patio, dressed in flowered boxer shorts and a whistle on a string wrapped around his neck. He held a clipboard and began announcing each event while the rest of us flopped underneath the shade of an apple tree. We rolled our eyes. We wiped the sweat from our brows.

"The potato sack races will begin in one minute." Dad called out as he began passing out burlap bags. My mother stood by, trying not to laugh as she poured a cool drink into paper cups at a nearby picnic table.

Then it happened. My little sister, Annie, then about ten, stood up and said, "It's too hot!"

With that, all my brothers and sisters angrily tossed aside their potato sacks, their voices rising in our backyard like thick smoke from a raging fire.

"This is stupid. I'm not running in this heat," my older sisters cried out.

"My friends are playing baseball. I hate throwing Jarts!" my younger brother shouted.

I watched in amazement. I'd never seen the likes of this.

My brothers and sisters were actually showing anger toward my father. This was unprecedented. This was a family insurrection, a backyard mutiny, an uprising of children against father.

"I don't want to throw water balloons!" I yelled as I threw my sack, my voice joining the angry mob.

Dad calmly lit up a Camel cigarette. He waited until everyone had gotten a chance to vent. Just waited. Then he did something he'd never done before. He conceded. He moved the orange construction cones to the shade. That Fourth of July, we ran the race—but in the shade.

To this day, my brothers and sisters still laugh about the SULLIVAN OLYMPIAD. At family gatherings, we've told and retold that story a hundred times over. It's the memory that we've titled "the day we got mad at Dad."

I think we cherish the memory because on that hot afternoon, our relationship with Dad changed forever. It was the first time we ever countered our father's authority. To our amazement, Dad "heard us out." In doing so, Dad acknowledged that we were growing up—that our thoughts and opinions had merit and that he loved us. It was okay to be mad. Years later, when Sarah was born, I was reminded that honest anger, expressed in love, changes things.

I sat in a rocking chair in our living room, cradling Sarah in a blanket, our Christmas tree twinkling. Outside our small home, the snow whirled softly, like feathers spinning in the wind. Though I was wearing a thick sweatshirt and fur slippers that looked like leopard skin, I shivered. With my husband gone Christmas shopping, the house was quiet and still.

A few weeks earlier, we had brought our newborn home from the hospital. Ever since then, our phone had been ringing nonstop and we had had a steady stream of visitors. Countless friends and relatives had dropped by, all of them bearing gifts for our family: a tuna-noodle casserole, a handmade baby blanket, a lovingly composed card or letter.

You've been chosen by God…

Your child is special…

"The Lord knows you can handle this," our loved ones would say as they offered consolation and took turns holding our newborn child. Although I appreciated their words of comfort and I understood that most everyone wanted to offer their heartfelt support, secretly, I was growing weary of hearing how "blessed" we were. Now that we were parents of a Down syndrome child, it seemed that our family had been instantaneously elevated to sainthood.

I leaned back in the rocker as Sarah slept in my arms. With so many guests to tend to, I hadn't had time to process the "bigness" of her disability.

"I don't want to be a saint," I said with a sigh. I closed my eyes. I fast-forwarded my thoughts through the years that lay ahead. *She won't learn to dance or sing…she'll never hold a job…she won't go to the prom.*

I thought of all the new mothers I had met during my recent stay in the hospital maternity ward; young mothers like me who had given birth to healthy babies without disabilities.

I wish I were a normal mom.

Seconds later, the doorbell rang. Balancing Sarah in the crook of one arm, I opened the front door with the other.

"Hey, Sis," my younger sister, Annie, called out as a whoosh of cold wind blew into our entryway. A natural beauty in her early twenties, Annie was still single and un-attached, working as a businesswoman in a fashionable office. With her chestnut brown hair coated with snowflakes, Annie stepped inside, stomping the snow from her boots. She handed me a small gift wrapped in shiny pink paper.

"Lose the shoes," she joked, as she pointed to my animal-print slippers. She wanted to make me laugh. I could only give her a halfhearted grin.

"Let me hold my sweetie," Annie said, as she quickly snatched Sarah from my arms. My sister's presence brought untold comfort to me. I knew I could share my truest feelings with her.

"Sarah...look at the pretty ornaments," Annie said gleefully, as she drew near to our Christmas tree, dancing merrily as she rocked Sarah. As I began peeling away the pink wrapping from the present, I found a wooden name plaque carved with the words: *Sarah, God's Princess.*

I set the plaque down on the coffee table. I turned away from my sister, trying to fight back tears. "I am the mother of a handicapped child. This is my new identity," I told her.

Annie looked out the window, her thoughts far away. "Nancy, maybe God allowed Sarah's birth to teach you something," she said.

I looked at her, indignant. It was easy for her to say. How could she ever understand what I was going through? Didn't she know that Sarah's disability had brought unspeakable heartache into my life?

"Teach me something? Teach me something?" I felt my face flush with anger. I drew near to the front door and opened it. "I think it's time for you to leave!" I told Annie.

Annie maintained her composure. "You're not mad at me...you're mad at God," she said. Annie gave Sarah a kiss and placed her in my arms. As she put on her coat, Annie reached into her pocket and handed me a small card that bore the name and phone number of a therapist named Jack. "I got his name at church. Everyone says he's a great counselor. He has a son with a disability," she told me.

The next morning, while Sarah took her nap, I called Jack. "I have a cancellation for tomorrow; come see me then," Jack suggested.

The following afternoon, I met Jack for the first time in the lobby of his second-floor office. After greeting me in the lobby, he handed me a cup of coffee and guided me into a counseling room furnished with a plaid couch and a couple of overstuffed chairs. The walls of the room were lined with shelves of family photos and neatly arranged books. I saw a framed picture of a boy in a wheelchair and several titles about theology and faith.

"Welcome," Jack said, as he motioned for me to sit on the couch. I guessed that he was in his fifties, a lanky man with long gray hair pulled back into a ponytail. That day he wore a tweed jacket, blue jeans, and wire-rimmed glasses.

I sat down, nestling myself into one corner of the couch. Jack sat right across from me, a notebook in his lap, and a pen in his hand. "Why are you here?" he asked, his tone efficient and matter of fact.

I folded my hands. I looked at the clock that hung on a wall by the bookcase. I wanted to leave. "I'm here…I'm here because my baby has Down syndrome," I said.

"How does that feel?" Jack asked.

I took a deep breath. "It feels hard…," I heard myself say.

"Why is it hard?" Jack asked.

A wave of sadness rushed over me. There were so many reasons to be sad. Instead of experiencing the joys of becoming a new mother, I was wondering if my baby would ever walk or talk. I was scared about the future. The doctors were hinting that she might need open-heart surgery. I had so many questions; so many painful questions that no one could answer. *Would our finances be affected? Would we have to place her in an institution? Would we be able to have other children? Would I ever laugh again?*

"Sarah is a beautiful child. God gave her to me...." I didn't want Jack to think I didn't love my child.

Jack's gaze was intent. "Why is it hard?" he repeated.

I tried not to make eye contact with Jack. How could I tell him how I really felt? I had been raised Catholic. I had been brought up to believe that sacrifice was part of life; that serving others was noble and that suffering was the mark of a true Christian. I began remembering the day I was confirmed. Back then I was in the ninth grade. I sat in the front row of our church, surrounded by young Catholic classmates; the girls donned in white dresses and the boys dressed in dark jackets. "You are now soldiers of Christ. In life you will bear many crosses. Offer them up to God," the bishop had proclaimed from the pulpit.

"Nancy, your baby is handicapped. Why is that hard?" Jack asked, prying me away from my thoughts.

"It's hard...." I paused. "My baby is different. She will always be different."

Jack nodded as if he understood.

"But God made her that way, it was his will...," I added in haste.

Jack jotted down a few notes. "Why do you think Sarah's birth was God's will?"

I knew that Sarah's disability was the result of a genetic abnormality. There was a scientific explanation for her condition, "an extra chromosome," the doctors had explained. Still ever since Sarah's birth, I'd been questioning God's role in genes and chromosomes and genetic anomalies.

Why would an all-powerful, all-knowing, all-loving God allow a child to be born with so many imperfections?

"I love my baby," I told Jack.

The room was quiet. I could hear the radiator clicking. My jaw began to tighten up. I bit my lip. I was completely unprepared for the fountain of anger that was beginning to rise up inside of me. I curled my hands into tight fists.

"I think I'm mad...," I whispered softly, trying to disguise what I was feeling.

"Who are you mad at?" Jack persisted.

"I don't know," I said. I knew I wasn't mad at Annie, but why had I blown up at her? Who was there to be mad at? There was no one to blame.

Jack persisted. "Nancy, who are you mad at?"

I looked at Jack before I spoke. "God allowed Sarah to be born...."

A long silence followed.

"I'm mad at God...." Even as I spoke the words, I wanted to take them back. *How could I be angry at almighty God?*

Jack took a deep breath. I could tell that he was carefully calculating what he would say next. "You and God must be good friends," he said.

I looked at him quizzically. I didn't understand what he was saying.

"Only close friends can share anger." With that, Jack looked at the clock. An hour had passed. "Nancy, we've made progress today. I'll see you next week," he said. I wanted to prolong the conversation, but it was time to leave.

The next day, I found myself pondering my conversation with Jack. Being angry with God—this was something new for me. Throughout my life, I had held a belief that life's trials should be accepted without resistance; without question. But Sarah's birth was forcing me to question my faith in a way I never had before.

Was it really okay to "have it out" with God? I wondered.

The week passed quickly. Then, on a snowy afternoon, a day before my next counseling session, I drove to the drugstore to buy diapers and formula. Sarah dozed in her car seat while I slowed down at a red stoplight. From my windshield, I noticed a school bus that was stopped at a nearby corner. I watched as child after child got off that bus. They were beautiful children, all of them bundled in knitted scarves and mittens, happily skipping and romping through the snow as they raced toward their neighborhood homes. Most of the little girls had ponytails and braids that trailed from their caps. One little boy carried a black trumpet case.

I began counting the children, "One…two…seven…ten…thirteen…," as they scurried past my car. The light turned green. Instead of driving to the store, I steered my car into an empty parking lot that overlooked an outdoor skating rink.

I got out of my car and leaned against the door. The snow kept falling. "God…why *my* child?" I shouted, my voice echoing through the empty parking lot. No one was around. I lifted my glance toward heaven. "I'm mad at you…I'm mad at *you!*" my voice becoming louder with each acclamation.

The winter wind felt cold and bitter. Eyes now misting, I got back into the car, shivering. Just then, Sarah looked over at me from her car seat. She smiled, and then fell back asleep.

"This is hard," I told God. For the first time in my life, I was being truly honest with God. I wasn't being a stalwart soldier of Christ. I wasn't pretending that this cross of raising a handicapped child was easy to bear. I wasn't "offering up" my suffering. I was only being what I was, a frightened first-time mother of a Down syndrome child. It hurt.

I glanced at my daughter sleeping in her car seat. I recalled a passage from Psalm 139, one that I had read often during my pregnancy: "You have searched me and known me... / for it was you who formed my inward parts; / you knit me together in my mother's womb" (v 1, 13).

With mittened hands, I brushed the small face of my Down syndrome baby. Even before her birth, God had fashioned every detail of her being. He had "knit together" her "inward parts," her genes and chromosomes, her intellectual potential, even her limited capacity to think and feel.

A gust of snow whirled over my windshield as I imagined God sitting between me and my baby, his arms stretching over us like a protective canopy. "I made both of you..." I could almost hear God say.

In that moment, I allowed myself to feel the depth of my hurt, my disappointment, even my anger. These were sacred responses, holy emotions, the gifts of my inward being.

It was okay to be mad at God. My relationship with the Lord was secure. I was beginning to understand that true faith is not dependent on questions that are answered, but on believing God's love remains, even when no answers come.

Later that evening, while Don watched Sarah at home, I drove to Annie's apartment. She greeted me at the door, wearing a bathrobe and puffy, sequined slippers. "I'm so glad you came. I was just doing my nails...let's have some coffee," she said.

We talked late into the night about faith, true friendship, and the power of being honest with God.

"I'm sorry I blew up at you. It was 'misplaced anger,'" I told my sister in a joking tone, my self-diagnosis sounding like I was a seasoned psychologist.

Annie knew exactly what I was saying, "God already knew you were mad."

When at last our time together came to a close, I looked down at Annie's feet. Her sequined slippers looked like two shimmering disco balls. I couldn't resist. "Lose the shoes," I told her. We laughed.

Ponderings

> *anger: ang'ger, n. Originally grief. Anger, grief,*
> *sorrow, to grieve.* (New Webster Encyclope-
> dic Dictionary of the English Language.)

God gave each of us the capacity to feel anger. Though it's a complex emotion, one that needs to be expressed appropriately, anger forces us to ask tough questions and to deal with our deepest griefs and sorrows.

In Psalm 13, King David challenges God with painful questions as he wanders in a barren desert, hiding out from his enemies. "How long, O LORD? Will you forget me forever? / How long will you hide your face from me? / How long must I bear pain in my soul, / and have sorrow in my heart all day long?" (v. 1–2).

If King David questioned God, so can we. Perhaps you are going through your own desert experience—a time of unexpected hardship or loss. Maybe your adversity is triggering by some anger.

Go ahead. Give yourself permission to hurt. Start asking God questions, even if no answers come. Let your anger validate the security you feel in God's presence and the deeply personal friendship you share with your Creator. There is such a thing as Holy Anger. "Offer it up" to God.

Only then can true healing begin.

THREE

Don't Suffer Alone

The church was dimly lit with votive candles that flick-
ered on the altar. It was the third Saturday in the month
of January, late in the afternoon. With the temperature dip-
ping well below freezing, the church was mostly empty, except for a few people praying the rosary or reading prayer
books. The cold and snow didn't keep our family away. Like
every third Saturday, our family was there to attend confession.

Amid my parents and other siblings, I sat in the back
row, right next to my sister Peggy. Nearby, was a "confessional," a small boxy room that looked like a telephone
booth. I felt dread.

"We committed a sin," I whispered to Peggy.

"Just a little one," she replied softly.

A few days earlier, as the snow fell over our neighborhood, the two of us had walked home from school, the aroma
of just-baked cookies greeting us as we opened our front
door. While Peggy and I unbundled ourselves from mittens
and jackets, our heavyset grandmother, "Marma," handed
us a plate brimming with date cookies.

"How bout a treat?" she asked.

Marma was our father's mom. When she came to visit

our family from California, she often stayed for six months at a time.

"She has a disease…she forgets things. Be patient with her," my father had told us time and time again.

Marma forgot lots of things, our names, the address of our home, where her bedroom was located. Peggy and I could never figure out why she always remembered an eighty-year-old recipe that had never been written down. Every afternoon, Marma baked up a fresh batch from memory. Peggy and I hated date cookies.

"Gee, thanks Marma," I said, feigning delight.

"Mmmmm," Peggy replied, as she took the plate into her hands and the two of us made our way down the hall to the room we shared as sisters. We set the cookies on the dresser and flopped on our beds. We watched the steam rise from the heavy, oatmeal-laden confections.

"The dates look like crickets," I told Peggy.

With that, my sister opened the window as a rush of cold winter wind filled our room.

"I can't…I can't eat another one…," Peggy declared.

She grabbed a cookie from the plate. She took aim, flinging it out the window like she was tossing a Frisbee. I followed her lead. Winding up, I threw a cookie, full force, until it hit the neighbor's snow-covered birdbath.

We laughed on our beds, holding our hands over our mouths so Marma couldn't hear. One by one we threw every date cookie, giggling uncontrollably as the homemade treats ricocheted into snowbanks, bushes, and trees.

Now, as Peggy and I sat together in church, I knew our day of reckoning had come.

"I'll go first," I told Peggy, as I made my way to the booth and the confessional door closed behind me with a thud.

I knelt down on wooden kneelers that creaked. It was dark, all except for a small screen where the silhouette of a priest was lit by a small bulb.

"Father...I've sinned. I threw Marma's cookies in the snow," I told the pastor, my hands folded in repentance.

The priest tried to hold back his chuckles. I could see his shoulders shaking through the screen. "Next time...eat the cookies. It's a sacrifice that will please God."

After Peggy's confession, the two of us met in the back of the church, discussing the penance we had received.

"We gotta eat 'em," I told my sister.

"We gotta suffer," Peggy whispered.

For the next two months, Peggy and I ate date cookies every afternoon in our room. In between chews of dates and swallows of oatmeal chunks, we laughed. We were in this together. We understood each other's pain. Our "suffering" was easier to bear because we were sharing it.

Years later, in the early months of Sarah's life, I began understanding why I never forgot those date cookie afternoons. Even though Peggy and I were very young, we had learned an immutable truth about life. No one should ever suffer alone. I would remember this truth during Sarah's infancy, especially during the lonely days that marked her open-heart surgery.

It was a Sunday afternoon in March, two weeks before Easter. My father stood in the kitchen of my childhood home, slicing ham for sandwiches at the counter. At fifty-four years of age, Dad still looked like a giant, his massive arms bulging from the sleeves of his yellow golf shirt.

In a nearby living room, my husband and brothers and in-laws watched a game of basketball on TV. I sat at the kitchen table with my five grown sisters; my mother holding Sarah in her arms.

"Let me hold Sarah… No, it's my turn," my sisters argued.

My mother tightened her "grandmotherly grip" over my baby. "She's mine for now," my mom quipped.

Though I was surrounded by family, I was preoccupied. In just a few weeks, Sarah would be undergoing a risky open-heart surgery. The doctors had discovered two holes in her heart and a valve that needed repair.

"Nancy, I brought something for you," my sister Peggy said. She reached into her purse and pulled out a card. Annie leaned over as I opened the envelope. Soon, I began reading aloud the quote on the card: "Do not pray for an easy life, pray to be a strong person."

Annie raised her eyebrows. "I don't know about that card. If I had my choice, I'd opt for an easy life," Annie replied.

My sister "Julie" patted me on the back. She looked at Sarah lying in my mother's arms. "You aren't alone," she said.

Soon, my father drew near, setting a plate of snacks on the table. He glanced at the card. "Nancy," he said, as he began chewing on a sandwich. He nodded his head toward Sarah. "You've got to remember…she's not just your kid, she's all of ours."

I looked at my father. Though he had a tough exterior, Sarah's birth had been hard on him. Deep down, I knew that Dad wanted to make the pain of Sarah's disability disappear, but he couldn't. Instead, he just stood there, his protective presence, hovering.

"Thanks Dad…that means a lot," I said.

I had the support of my entire family. Their ongoing encouragement was like a candle of hope that never stopped flickering, even in this dark time of doubt and uncertainty. Even so, I couldn't help but feel alone.

No one really understands what this is like, I told myself.

Weeks later, on a morning in late spring, Sarah lay in a hospital crib framed with steel flats that looked like mirrors.

Above her a sign read: Sterilized Area. Our daughter's heart surgery was over, but now she was in the intensive care unit and her recovery was dragging into weeks. Don and I were taking turns keeping a constant vigil over her bedside.

Earlier that morning, I had sent my husband home to take a nap. Though I was exhausted, I sat by Sarah's crib and held her tiny hand. I could smell alcohol and Betadine. Her little body was covered with breathing tubes and bandages. I felt alone as the monitor above recorded each of her heartbeats with a wavy line.

The doctors drew near to her crib. They murmured softly and wrote on clipboards. "We need to do some tests. It will take a few hours," they told me.

Quietly slipping out of intensive care, I made my way down a hallway toward a lobby lined with chairs. I bought a leathery apple from a vending machine. I sat down and tried to read a magazine. Other parents were in that lobby; parents just like me—parents whose children suffered from cancer or heart disease or ailments so rare that I had never heard of them. I couldn't help but overhear their stories. I wondered if God was listening, too.

While I turned on a TV that was mounted near the ceiling, a tall bearded man walked into the lobby. He was holding the hand of a little boy. He wore the distinctive clothing of an Orthodox Jew; a tall dark hat with a brim, a long coal-colored coat with tails, and black tapered trousers. Curious, I watched as he placed a shawl and a small prayer book on his son's lap. Then he looked up and gave me a quick nod in greeting.

"My name is Shimon," the man told me. A rabbi, Shimon had flown in from Boston that morning. "I'm staying with a Jewish community right here in the area," he said. He went on to explain that his son had a serious kidney disease. "He needs a transplant," Shimon explained.

I introduced myself and began telling him about Sarah. "It's been hard," I said.

As the days passed, Shimon turned that lobby into a sort of living room. He set a gold-framed picture of his family on a table next to the vending machine. Each morning, he offered me kosher food from a brown paper bag; fresh-baked bread, red grapes, seasoned fish. And every morning he put on the shawl and his yarmulke. Then with his prayer book opened, he would recite several Hebrew prayers in a soft voice.

Whenever he prayed, I watched something amazing happen in the lobby. One by one, each parent turned away from their magazines and candy bars and TV talk shows. Together we bowed our heads. Most of us had come from Christian traditions, yet each of us felt a certain strength, a quiet comfort as he prayed.

In between those prayers and the breaking of bread, Shimon and I shared conversation. We talked of the cold Midwestern winters, the ocean breezes in Boston, our families, and God. Shimon spoke of the great "I AM," an inextinguishable fire that led his people out of darkness, a brilliant flame that blazed in times of uncertainty. He was at peace with God.

I, on the other hand, kept thinking about all the children who were undergoing painful medical treatments and all the heartbroken parents who, amid unbearable sorrow, were trying to be strong.

"It's not right," I told Shimon. "Why does God allow such suffering?" Shimon just listened.

Then, early one Sunday morning, Sarah took a turn for the worse. The doctors discovered a staph infection in her blood. It could take her life. While my husband and I stood by her crib, she lay almost lifeless, her little body bruised from weeks of incisions, needles, and stitches. Like the other children in that intensive care ward, she had battled more disease in a few short weeks than most people do in a lifetime.

As I held her tiny ashen hand, I retreated to a dark, despairing place where the light of faith is snuffed out and God's absence seems real.

"Where are you?" I asked God. Then I made my way to the lobby and buried my head in my hands. *I don't want to be a strong person.*

"Can I help you?" I heard a voice ask. I looked up and saw the rabbi; he had taken a seat right across from me.

"Shimon," I asked, "How can God allow such suffering?"

For a moment, Shimon bowed his head. Then he turned to me and said something I will never forget. "I do not know much about the God you hold in your heart," he began, "except that he suffered and died on a cross. Perhaps it is your suffering God who draws near to you now."

As he spoke, images of Calvary began to fill my mind—the somber sky, the nails of iron, the cross. I could almost feel a wounded Christ wrap his injured arms around me, my sick baby, my husband, Shimon, and every parent in that lobby. I could almost hear God saying, "I love Sarah. She's not just yours…she's mine, too."

Soon a warmth began to fill me. It started out as an ember of hope; then became a blaze of faith. God was present. I knew it. I felt it.

Three days later, Sarah recovered from the infection that threatened her life. Days later, with suitcases packed to leave the hospital, our family passed through the lobby one last time. Cradling my baby, I searched for Shimon to say goodbye. He wasn't there. Some of the other parents happily reported that a kidney had been found for Shimon's son. "He'll be in surgery all morning," they told us.

I scrawled a quick thank-you note on the back of a candy box and tucked it underneath Shimon's family picture.

When we arrived home from the hospital, my mother, along with most of my siblings, were waiting for our arrival on the front porch of our house. My father wasn't there. He had passed away from a heart attack before Easter.

It doesn't seem right…Dad's not here, I thought to myself.

Even though my family was still grieving the loss of my father, muddling their way through feelings of sorrow, they had come together to celebrate Sarah's homecoming.

"It's good to be home," I told the clan. Holding Sarah, I walked into my living room and smelled the lemon scent of furniture polish.

Jeanne and Kathy, my older sisters, waved their dustcloths. "We cleaned everything," they said.

Julie guided me into the kitchen where a pizza casserole was cooking in the oven. "I made cookies, too," my sister Peggy said. She pointed to a plate of chocolate chip cookies on the counter. "No dates in those," she joked. I smiled.

While Don chatted with my brothers, Annie scooped

Sarah from my arms. With baby in tow, Annie led me to Sarah's room. Above my baby's crib was a homemade sign that Annie had taped to the wall. It read: Welcome Home, Princess Sarah.

"Remember…she's not just *your* kid, she's all of ours," Annie told me, as she laid Sarah down for a nap.

Soon Peggy and Julie drew near, the two of them tucking teddy bears into Sarah's crib. I hugged my two sisters.

"Dad is here…I know he is," Annie said.

I could feel my earthly father's presence—protective, comforting. I could also feel the warmth of my heavenly Father's love. Though everything in life was hard, strength was welling up inside of me. My family would always stay close, no matter what lay ahead.

And so would God.

Ponderings

suffering: *the bearing of pain, inconvenience, or loss; pain endured, distress.* (New Webster Encyclopedic Dictionary of the English Language.)

A few weeks back, our parish priest was presenting a homily on the topic of suffering.

"Every roof has its sorrow; every heart has its ache," he told our congregation. It's true. Everyone, at some point, experiences the "inconvenience" of unexpected pain or loss. Everyone has their own story of personal suffering. Loved ones get sick. People let us down. Relationships break apart. People we love pass away.

Though suffering is part of the human condition, we are never alone.

In the Book of Isaiah, we are comforted by these beautiful words:

> *When you pass through the waters, I will be with you; / and through the rivers, they shall not overwhelm you; / when you walk through fire you shall not be burned, / and the flame shall not consume you. / For I am the* LORD *your God, the Holy One of Israel, your savior"* (43:2–3).

Whatever suffering you are going through, remember, God understands. He is your true companion. He is your inextinguishable flame of faith, your ever-shining light of hope.

The great "I AM" is with you.

FOUR

Be Beautiful

The December sun streamed in through the corner windows of my maternal grandmother's kitchen. That winter morning, "Mema" and I were making a batch of licorice "anis" candy, a holiday recipe that my grandmother made every year.

At nine years old, with my hair tied back into a ponytail, I measured corn syrup into a measuring cup. Mema stood at the stove, stirring sugar and water in a pan as she twirled her wooden spoon round and round. With her short, gray hair waved into tight "pin curls," Mema wore a floral print dress with a full skirt, an apron tied around her waist.

"It's time to add the licorice," Mema said, as she turned down the heat on the stove. She reached into a cupboard and handed me a tiny plastic bottle trimmed with a red label.

"This is my favorite part," I told Mema, as I opened the bottle, just to breathe in the scent of the familiar spice. "It smells like Christmas."

My grandmother stood in the sunlight; her gray hair glistening like exquisite silver jewelry. Her twinkling eyes shown brightly beneath thick, bifocal glasses. The lines on her face all curved upward, like perfectly shaped arches.

"Mema...your wrinkles...they look like smiles," I told her. Mema laughed as she wiped her hands on her apron. "Nancy, wrinkles are beauty marks. Don't ever forget that," she said.

In that moment, I took a "mental snapshot" of Mema. Even though I was very young, I knew I wanted to remember exactly how she looked that day; the way the sunlight lit her aging smile, the love and tenderness that radiated from her furrowed face. I didn't just "see" her beauty, I felt it.

When I became Sarah's mother, years later, I discovered that my baby had inherited one of Mema's best qualities. Sarah was beautiful, too.

After weeks in the intensive care unit, it felt wonderful to bring Sarah home. At last, she was on the mend; her little heart repaired. I was ready for life to be a little less intense. I was looking forward to getting to know my baby without the pressures of looming medical procedures and surgeries.

Though Sarah's surgery had been difficult; emotionally, physically, and spiritually, I had gained a whole new appreciation for my daughter's life. Sarah was strong. She had made it through a risky operation. She had recovered from respiratory failure. She had defied a life-threatening infection.

After coming so close to losing her, I was beginning to realize how much I loved her. Now that we were home, I relished the simple routines of mothering her. I cherished the littlest things; taking her for walks in a stroller, feeding her a bottle on the couch, listening to her laugh when I tucked her into her crib.

Sarah always smiled. Always. Her sweet countenance

brightened my life, even though, at ten months ol[
velopmental delays were becoming more obvious.

Unlike other infants, Sarah hadn't yet mastered the basic milestones of learning how to sit up or crawl. In addition to her mental limitations, her cardiac problems had set her back in all areas of development. Nonetheless, I was optimistic. Her open-heart surgery was over. It was time to help her become all that she could become. It was time to take advantage of all the community programs that were available to our family.

A couple of weeks after we brought Sarah home from her surgery, a community social worker named Maggie dropped by for a visit. That afternoon, I greeted her at our front door, holding Sarah in my arms.

Maggie was in her early thirties; petite, with curly red hair and light-filled eyes that radiated a zest for life. That day, she showed up carrying a beach ball and a red bag filled with toys.

"You look like Mary Poppins," I joked.

Maggie chuckled as I led her into our living room and she began setting up small toys and equipment on my carpet. "May I hold Sarah?" Maggie asked. I placed my baby in her arms. "She's so beautiful. Look at her sparkling eyes," Maggie said. "She must be Irish."

I immediately trusted Maggie. As she held my baby, the two of us sat together on our living room carpet, exchanging casual introductions. Maggie's family had recently moved to Minnesota from the West Coast.

"I love this area, there's so many lakes and green trees," she said. Her enthusiasm for her job was infectious. "Sarah will do great things. She'll surprise you...just wait and see," Maggie said.

I hung on Maggie's every word as she began explaining why she had brought the beach ball.

"Over the next few weeks, we're going to work on building Sarah's muscle tone," she said. I watched as Maggie carefully placed little Sarah on top of the ball, tummy side down.

"Watch closely," Maggie said, as she held Sarah's back firmly and began gently rocking the ball to and fro. Each time the ball moved forward, Sarah lifted her head. "See, she's using her neck muscles," Maggie said.

Though it was a small accomplishment, one that most babies achieve in their earliest weeks, I was elated. I patted my daughter on the back. "Great job, Sarah."

In the weeks that followed, Maggie visited our home every Wednesday afternoon. In time, she taught Sarah how to shake a rattle, how to grip, roll and throw a small ball, how to maintain eye contact with a toy train that rattled around a small track.

I appreciated Maggie's input. Every week, she gave me a list of developmental "assignments" to complete with Sarah: blow bubbles from a wand, repeat the alphabet, build towers out of blocks.

Maggie was helping me to see that the everyday interactions I had with my baby were significant. She was showing me that the simple act of playing with Sarah, talking to her, making eye contact with her, cuddling her, all these little things were going to make a huge difference in her development.

One afternoon when Maggie arrived for her Wednesday visit, I lead her into Sarah's room. "Look, Maggie...look," I said proudly, pointing to Sarah. My daughter was sitting up all by herself; smiling as she stacked blocks on the floor.

"You did it, Sarah...you did it," Maggie exclaimed as she knelt down to hug my daughter. Sarah beamed.

Then Maggie reached into her red bag and handed me a coupon for a free portrait at a local photo studio. "Get a good picture of Sarah," Maggie said. "You'll want to remember these precious days."

My thoughts began to drift. During the first months of Sarah's life, I had tried taking her to a photographer. On that morning, I had dressed Sarah in a tiny yellow dress trimmed with embroidery and lace. I had fastened a little Velcro bow to a lock of her baby-fine hair. While I sat in the waiting area of the photo studio, Sarah lay in my arms looking like a lifeless doll, her heart problems triggering noticeable weakness and fatigue.

I saw other young mothers who had dressed their cherub-faced babies in fluffy dresses, bow ties and brimmed hats with ribbons. As I sat there, it was easy to see the physical resemblance between each mother and child. I looked down at the newborn baby I was holding in my arms. She had all the telltale signs of Down syndrome—slanted eyes, flaccid muscles, and soft palms.

Sarah was part of me, my own flesh and blood. We were mother and daughter. Still, her face bore no similarities to mine, or my husband's, or anyone in my family.

Her appearance shouldn't be important, I thought, even as my eyes began to well up. *I can't do this...not now...not today.* I left the studio with quick steps, hugging my baby protectively. *Good mothers don't feel this way.*

While driving home, I kept trying to figure out why the simple experience of visiting a photographer had brought such heartache.

Sarah slept in her car seat. *A photo tells the truth.* I suddenly knew exactly why I couldn't bring myself to take Sarah's picture. A baby picture would confirm and record my daughter's undeniable disability, a disability I was desperately trying to deny.

"I'm sorry, Sarah," I whispered. "I'm sorry, God."

Now, so many months later, I sat next to Sarah as she happily stacked her blocks. I turned my glance toward Maggie. "A few months ago, I tried taking Sarah to a photographer, but I couldn't do it," I told Maggie.

"Was it too hard?" Maggie asked.

Memories from my childhood began to surface. My family had always gotten a lot of attention. In their younger days, my parents were both head-turning handsome. In the early 1950s, Dad had played football for Notre Dame, a popular Irish athlete known on campus for his humor and wit. My mother, an avid reader of poetry and an accomplished seamstress, had been a cheerleader and runner up for homecoming queen.

During my growing-up years, my five sisters and I had gotten a lot of attention as well. We, too, were cheerleaders and class queens who had ridden in parades, waving to crowds from foil-trimmed floats. We were artists, storytellers, and comedians; popular with our peers.

My brothers were handsome athletes, high-school hockey stars who had often been featured in newspapers and on TV. The three of them had received scholarships at a prestigious Catholic college on the East Coast.

"There's the Sullivans…look at those kids," people would whisper Sunday mornings as our family filed into church, the eleven of us barely fitting into one wooden pew.

"Sarah has her own beauty," Maggie said, as my adolescent memories began to fade.

"Look at her face," Maggie continued. "Have you ever seen eyes that shine like hers?"

I looked into my baby's eyes. *They look like two candles.*

Sarah giggled as I placed a large block on top of her block tower, toppling it over.

"When Sarah smiles, there's a dimple on her left cheek …that's an angel's kiss," Maggie said, as she pointed to my grinning daughter.

Maggie took a pen and a small pad of paper from her bag and wrote down my "assignment" for the week: Take Sarah's picture.

A few days later, Sarah and I drove to the same photography studio that we had hastily left a few months earlier. This time as the two of us waited in the lobby, Sarah was the center of attention. My daughter looked like a princess; sitting on my lap—her puffy pink dress trimmed with eyelet; her red-tinted hair combed into one small ponytail that sprouted sweetly from the top of her head. Though there were other mothers and children in that lobby, Sarah stole the show.

"What a pretty dress you have."

"I love your ponytail."

"Oh, you look so lovely," each young mom told my baby.

Sarah smiled and waved. With every comment, her eyes shimmered.

A few days later, when I got the photo proofs back, I laid them all out on our kitchen table. *They are all so cute*, I told myself. I took one of the proofs into my hand—a snapshot of Sarah with her hands folded over her pink dress. She was grinning with glee, almost laughing. The dimple on her left cheek looked as if someone had painted it there.

There's something about this picture, I thought to myself. With the photo still in my hand, I made my way up our living room stairway, into our attic. I began sifting through

a cardboard box that contained memorabilia from my childhood: baptismal certificates, school report cards, old Christmas cards written by my grandmother. Paging through a
timeworn scrapbook, I found a black-and-white photo of
me when I was about six months old. There, on my right
cheek, as clear as could be, was a dimple.

I put Sarah's picture right next to mine, my eyes happily
dashing back and forth from my photo to hers. That dimple
was a definitive mark, one that affirmed our mother-daugh-
ter genes. Still, I was elated for another reason. As Sarah's
mom, I knew I had reached a milestone.

I kept looking at Sarah's photo. I realized that I was trea-
suring her appearance, embracing it, appreciating the beauty
marks that set her apart from all other children—the twinkle
in her slanted eyes, the sincerity of her low-toned smile, the
luster of her wavy, Irish-red hair.

She's so beautiful, I told myself, my glance still fixed on
the photo image of her face.

I was overjoyed. I couldn't stop smiling. Sarah and I would
always be bonded by something more important than common genes and distinguishing family features. It was love.

Ponderings

beauty: *qualities that delight the eye, the ear,
or the mind; loveliness, elegance, grace.* (New
Webster Encyclopedic Dictionary of the English Language.)

Most of us, at one time or another, have felt insecure about
our appearance. Maybe that's because we live in a world
where beauty is often defined by TV and magazine images

of porcelain-skinned models and chiseled-chinned men with bulging biceps.

Yet, Scripture tells us that we are made in the image and likeness of God. The Lord himself fashioned each of our faces, our bodies, our minds. In the forty-third chapter of Isaiah, God tells the children of Israel: "You are precious in my sight," (v. 4). Think, about that! When God looks at you, he sees what he has made. He is "delighted" with you, you are part of his family; his special child. Look around. Everyone you meet reflects the unique and creative beauty of God.

Just yesterday, as I drove from the grocery store, I looked out my car window and saw a touching sight. A little girl with pigtails was smiling as she steered her mobile wheel-chair down the street. She wasn't alone. Another little girl with long blonde hair was riding in the back of the wheel-chair, holding a soccer ball. The two of them were smiling, talking, laughing. They were simply sharing their lives; enjoying each other's presence.

They are both so beautiful, I told myself.

God made those little girls in his image. He made Sarah in his image. He made everyone in his image—you, me, the handicapped, the elderly, the infirmed, the gorgeous ones. We are all lovely, elegant and full of grace. We are bearers of heaven's beauty. In God's eyes, we are precious to behold.

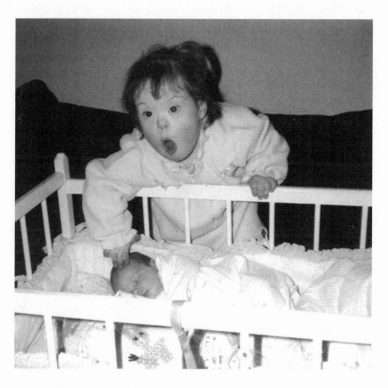

Three-year-old Sarah welcoming her new sister, "T. T."

FIVE

Call Everyone by Name

In the summer of 1964, I was eight years old and my youngest brother, Timmy, was just a baby. His little cherub body was chubby, the creases on his arms and legs looked like rubber bands. Much to my mother's delight, I didn't mind keeping Timmy occupied for hours at a time. I carried him with me everywhere, lugging him in the crook of my hip. I read him Dr. Suess books. I rocked him to sleep. Wherever I went, he went.

One summer night right after dinner, I put Timmy in a stroller and wheeled him out to the front of the house. While I sprayed mosquito repellent over his chunky arms, my siblings, along with countless kids from the neighborhood, began gathering for a nightly a game of kickball. That night there were probably about sixty of us.

My older sisters, Jeanne and Kathy, took their designated places on opposite sides of the street. Dressed in bib overalls and baseball caps turned backwards, they were the "elders" among us—the self-appointed captains of each team.

One by one, they began calling out names: "Johnny," Jeanne shouted, as my younger brother, blonde and brawny, strutted arrogantly to the curbside.

"Janet," Kathy called out, as the girl next door took her

place at Kathy's side. Janet had long blonde braids and strong legs. And, she was the best pitcher on our block.

The choosing of teams took about twenty minutes as Jeanne and Kathy continued to call out our nicknames: "Smokey...Piggy...Barrells." The teams grew larger and larger.

As usual, my name was last to be called, but I didn't mind. Timmy and I were a twosome. Though no one really wanted a baby on their team, there was no room for discrimination. Every night Dad always watched the game from our front porch, making sure that everyone got to play, even Timmy.

The game began. Soon it was my turn to kick. I stood at home plate waiting for the pitcher to roll the ball my way. I kicked the ball towards third base. Then I grabbed the handle of Timmy's stroller. I took off running, reeling Timmy's stroller around the bases, past first and second. My ponytail waved in the wind. With every bump and turn of the stroller, Timmy's chuckles and chortles echoed down the street.

"Go, Timmy, go!" all the neighborhood kids shouted.

Though the kickball games of my youth are now just memories, back then I learned something that I've never forgotten. In the game of life, everyone should get a chance to play.

Sarah learned to walk at eighteen months old. On the day she took her first steps, my husband and I threw a party for her in our kitchen. I bought pink sprinkled cupcakes and strung streams of crepe paper over the ceiling. While Don stood by the kitchen table, looking ridiculous as he waved an oversized balloon and blew a kazoo, I stood a few feet away by the fridge, holding Sarah's hand.

"Okay, Sarah, this is it," I said. I rolled up the legcuffs on her bib overalls. I tied the laces of her tiny tennis shoes and adjusted her pink-framed glasses. She wiggled from my arms.

"Da...Da," Sarah stuttered, as she took a few steps on her own, wobbling, steadying herself as she made her way toward her dad.

With her hair combed into ribboned pigtails, Sarah smiled with every step. Don waved his balloon wildly. "C'mon, Sarah. You can do it," he called.

When at last she tumbled into his arms, I began jumping up and down like a teenage cheerleader. "Sarah, you're a superstar...you are...you are!" I said.

We clapped. We danced with Sarah by the stove. "Sarah ...Sarah...Sarah," Don and I chanted; the two of us sounding like loyal sports fans cheering on our favorite star. A shower of joy was raining down on our family, covering us with unimaginable happiness. Our elation was ugraspable.

There was no denying that Sarah's birth had brought a disproportionate measure of pain and peril to our lives. But now, the scales were tipping. Joy, such as we had never known, was bringing balance to the heartache we had known for so many months.

Sarah was walking. For Don and I, her first steps were like a resurrection. A whole new world of possibility had opened up for our daughter and for us. If she could learn to walk, she could learn to do other things. Our spirits soared.

After Sarah started walking, her development came slow, but it was sure and steady. She wanted to explore everything. She loved playing with the pots and pans in the kitchen cupboards, turning on the water in the bathroom, or trying on my shoes and dresses.

Every night, I would read to Sarah as she sat on my lap on the living room couch. Her favorite children's book was a colorful alphabet book, its pages decorated in large block letters and corresponding pictures.

Night after night, our routine was the same: "A is for apple," I would say, as I turned to the first page.

"Ah…Ah…Ahpull…" Sarah would repeat as she pointed to the picture.

Though speech was a challenge for Sarah, and she often stuttered, she persevered, pronouncing each word as best she could. While turning each page of the book, she would tackle each letter, tirelessly: "B-ba…bababy." Sometimes I would add my own comments, "Sarah, everything has a name. Isn't that neat?"

Now that I was a stay-at-home mom, I was discovering that I hadn't really left my teaching job. Each day with Sarah held countless opportunities to guide and instruct. It felt natural to teach Sarah.

"M-mom, w-what this? W-wha—w-hat—n-n-name?" Sarah would ask each day, as she smelled the soap in the bathroom or she stood on a chair, pouring cereal into a bowl. She wanted to speak. She wanted to learn.

One day while Sarah and I shared a picnic lunch at a nearby park, Sarah handed me a bologna sandwich. "What… n-name?" Sarah asked as she held the bread close to my face. I smelled mayonnaise. I felt nauseated. I didn't know why.

Over the next few days, I felt queasy every time I looked at food. I made an appointment to see the doctor. "You're pregnant," he said.

Don was thrilled with the news. "Sarah's going to have a

new sister or brother," he said, as the two of us sat at our kitchen table and Sarah played by the cabinets, scattering pots and pans over the floor.

Weeks earlier, Don and I had gone through genetic counseling. Though the medical experts had assured us that our odds of having another Down syndrome child were very slim, there were no guarantees that our future children would be born healthy.

"What if we have another handicapped child?" I asked Don, as Sarah clanged one of her pans with a wooden spoon.

"Mum...Mum...," Sarah said, as she waved to me, her eyes shining.

Though I couldn't imagine life without Sarah, a second pregnancy made me feel vulnerable.

Don scooped Sarah into his arms. "If we have another disabled kid...we'll deal with it. We'll get the help we need. We'll be okay," he said cuddling her tightly.

Don and I were at very different places. For me, the thought of having another disabled child sent me into a spiritual whirlwind.

As the early months of my pregnancy passed, I began examining my beliefs in a way I never had before. A Christian, I'd been taught that life begins at conception. I was grounded in the teachings I had learned. In college, I had taken a theology course, which explored moral topics like euthanasia, suicide, and abortion.

One afternoon, as our class discussed both sides of the abortion issue, my classmates, most of them Catholic women in their early twenties, began arguing with one another. "A woman's body is her own business....An unborn child has rights, too...What if a woman is pregnant with a handicapped child?" came the opposing views.

Our instructor, a Catholic nun, didn't make any judgments. She just made a lot of eye contact and listened to each opinion, respectfully. At the end of the class, she gave us an assignment. "Read Psalm 139. We'll discuss it next week," she said.

Later that night in my dorm room, I began reading the ancient passage:

> *...Wonderful are your works; / that I know very well. / My frame was not hidden from you, / when I was being made in secret, / intricately woven in the depths of the earth. / Your eyes beheld my unformed substance...* (Psalm 139:14–16).

Though it was hard to imagine, I rewound my thoughts back in time, to the very first moments of my own life. I closed my eyes and tried to envision myself, safe and warm in my mother's womb; an unborn baby just inches in measure. Under God's wondrous glance, I had been miraculously "fashioned"—my face, my eyes, even the fingerprints on my hand. *God watched over me,* I told myself.

That night as I held my Bible in my college bedroom, I made a private promise to myself and to God. Though I respected the opinions of others, I knew that I could never terminate a pregnancy without fighting a lifetime war with my conscience. God's creative plan for the unborn was sacred; infallible. If there were children in my future, I would say yes to them. I would always choose life.

I could've never imagined that a few years later, I would be the one to give birth to a handicapped child. Now that I was facing a second pregnancy, I was beginning to realize that "choosing life" required gut-wrenching bravery, not to mention a conviction that God never, ever makes mistakes.

I would say yes to this second baby, healthy or handicapped. For me, there was no other response that felt "righter." But it wouldn't be an easy yes.

While my second pregnancy wore on and my waistline expanded, I kept myself busy. I wallpapered the bathroom and stenciled vines on our living room walls. I enrolled Sarah in toddler "playtimes" and adaptive recreation classes. In the evenings, while Don watched Sarah, I took a quilting class and a writing course. I didn't want to give myself a minute to think about what life might be like if we had another handicapped child.

As I felt the first kicks of my unborn child, I tried not to become too attached to the life that was growing within me. "What if something goes wrong?" I lamented to Don.

His optimism was unwavering. "What if something goes right?" he replied.

When I was about six months along, we moved a small toddler's bed into Sarah's room. "Ba...ba...bed," Sarah said, as she jumped up and down on her new mattress, waving her hands with glee. The crib Sarah had slept in for so many months was now unoccupied, ready to welcome a new baby.

One night as my due date grew closer, I tucked Sarah into her new bed and began explaining that she would soon have a new baby brother or sister.

"Sarah, there's a baby right here...under my heart," I told her as I placed my hand on my tummy. I wasn't sure how much she would understand.

"W-what...what...name?" Sarah asked, as she pointed to my enormous belly. Don and I had talked about names, but I had been hesitant. I wasn't sure why I didn't want to make any final decisions on what we would call our child.

"We'll wait until the baby comes," I told her.

Sarah was persistent. "What...n-nn-n-name?" she insisted, as she patted my tummy.

"We still have some time to think about that," I said.

Then, just a few days before our baby was born, I got an unexpected phone call from Marie, an old college roommate. Though I hadn't seen Marie in years, we had kept in touch through the years by phone.

After graduating from college, Marie had made a lot of money as a businesswoman, climbing the ladder of success at a Fortune-500 company in another state. Recently, however, she had made a dramatic career change, moving back to Minnesota to accept a position as a director of a crisis pregnancy center.

"Let's have lunch. I'd love to see pictures of Sarah," Marie said.

The next day, I met Marie in the waiting area of a small café.

"You're pregnant again—that's absolutely wonderful. I love your maternity top," Marie said, hugging me. With her long dark hair pulled back into a silver clip, Marie, like always, looked slim and gorgeous. Dressed in a floral print dress and shiny black pumps, she hadn't aged a bit.

"Life must be treating you well," I told her, as we sat down and ordered our lunch.

"I love my job. It's so gratifying when a young, unwed mother chooses life," Marie said.

While the two of us caught up on our lives, I showed her snapshots of Sarah.

"You will never regret saying yes to her," Marie said. She

paused for a moment, her eyes fixed on mine. "When I was in college, I had an abortion...I never told anyone," she said.

Marie began sharing a story from her past, recounting the unrelenting depression she had experienced after making the decision to end her pregnancy.

"After I graduated, I became a workaholic. I didn't want to deal with my remorse. I threw myself into my work," she said.

Marie told of struggles with alcohol. She went to counselor after counselor. "I was hurting, but I kept telling myself... it couldn't be the abortion."

Eventually, Marie found healing in an unexpected place, at a large evangelical church in her neighborhood. There she enrolled in a nine-week postabortion course called CONQUERERS. During the course, she met several women like herself, who in a vulnerable moment had chosen abortion.

Marie remembered one of the sessions. "We were given a doll without a face. We were invited to take the doll home, to paint a face on the doll, and to name it." Marie fought back tears as she remembered the moment she had painted eyes on her doll. "My baby had a face," Marie said, as her words faded into a whisper.

I handed her a napkin. "It's okay," I told her.

After Marie regained her composure, she went on with her story, "I named my doll...my baby...Stephen...it means 'crowned one.'" Marie paused for a moment, taking in a deep breath. "When you name a child, you affirm their life."

As Marie spoke, I began understanding why my second pregnancy had been so hard on me. During the last few months, I had been thinking of my unborn child as a "something that could go wrong" rather than a special, sacred "someone" with a face—a name. Though I had said yes to my baby's life, I hadn't allowed myself to become emotionally attached to my child, to feel connected, to feel love. As I sat with Marie, I felt my baby kick.

"Stephen…that's a beautiful name," I told my friend.

Later that evening, while Sarah slept soundly in her toddler bed, Don and I sat at the kitchen table, paging through a small book of baby names. "I like Christina for a girl," I told my husband. Don turned to the section of the book that listed names that began with "C."

"Christina…Christopher…both of the names mean *follower of God*," Don said.

A week later, on a snowy February night, Christina Allison was born.

"It's a girl," our doctor happily called out as he took our brand-new baby and lifted her high so that Don and I could get a good look at her. "She's gunna break a lot of hearts," the doctor joked.

A sturdy-looking nurse with warm brown eyes and black "corn-rowed" hair stood by, taking it all in. She began wrapping Christina in small blankets as Don and I looked on. The nurse kept looking at me and then back at Christina. She shook her head to and fro, chuckling to herself. "I never saw a newborn who looks more like her mamma," she declared.

Later on, Don brought Sarah to the hospital for a visit. The next day, Don had combed her hair, pulling it back with mismatched barrettes, and dressed her in a little pink T-shirt that read: I'm the big sister.

Sarah sat on the edge of my bed, her eyes shimmering, happily swinging her legs as I tucked little Christina into her open arms.

"Mum…w-what n-name?" Sarah asked as she kissed her day-old sister. Sarah had waited such a long time to hear the name of this special someone she was now holding.

"Chris-T-ina…can you say that?" I asked my daughter as I took great effort to annunciate the letter "T."

Sarah tilted her head to the side as she struggled to pronounce the three-syllable word, "Chrisss…T…T…T…," Sarah said. It was just too hard for her. All at once, Sarah simplified the name we had chosen to her liking. "T. T.," she replied.

Don laughed. "Sarah, that's a *great* nickname," he said.

Sarah smiled proudly, rocking her new sister.

"What a gift," I said, as I looked at our new baby. Once again, joy such as we had never known, showered down on us like rain.

Like Sarah, our new daughter was real. She had a name. She was ours. Our elation was ungraspable.

Ponderings

name (nām): that by which a person is called or designated, in distinction from other persons or things. (New Webster Encyclopedic Dictionary of the English Language.)

Sarah's name means *God's princess*. My husband and I choose the name a few months before she was born, before we learned she was handicapped. Throughout the years, Sarah has lived up to her name, displaying a spiritual "regalness," passing on the glorious wisdom of God, her heavenly King.

Even in childhood, my daughter Sarah knew the importance of a name. She has taught me that names are powerful;

that names define us and affirm the miraculousness of our lives.

In Isaiah 43, God encourages his people with these words: "Do not fear, for I have redeemed you; / I have called you by name, you are mine" (v. 1).

The next time you have a few quiet moments, take a minute to close your eyes. Imagine yourself in the earliest stages of life—an unborn child—safe and warm in your mother's womb, just inches in measure. Imagine God watching over you, smiling. You hear his voice. He's calling out your name. He already knows who you are. What name do you hear?

What does your name mean? If you aren't sure, maybe it's time to find out. You may discover that your name says something about who you are in Christ, your unique gifts and talents, even your calling or mission on this earth.

SIX

Wear Your Crown

In the mid seventies, when I was a senior in high school, I was nominated for homecoming queen. I can still remember the school coronation like it was yesterday. That night, I stood with four other queen candidates on a brightly lit stage in our school auditorium. We wore different colored gowns. Our long dresses shimmered in the light. My mother had sewn my gown from orange satin-polyester that she had bought on sale, three yards for a dollar.

My hair was styled into a shoulder-length flip; my over-sprayed curls looked like orange juice cans. With my eyelids shadowed in blue, I prayed, *Please God, let me win the crown.*

The dean of students, "Mr. B," as we called him, walked to a microphone that was centered onstage. Wearing a plaid suit coat and slightly flared pants, he carried a sealed envelope; inside was the name of the newly elected queen. He drew near to a small table that was covered with a red velvet cloth. A crown was displayed on the table, a silver tiara covered with royal blue jewels.

"And now, the moment we've all been waiting for...," Mr. B proclaimed to the crowd that had gathered in the auditorium. "Sully...Sully...Sully," my teenage friends chanted

as they bellowed my nickname from all corners of the room.
A soft drum roll began. Mr B. opened the envelope. "Our
new homecoming queen is…"

It wasn't my name that was called.

That night, even though I congratulated the new queen
with a hug that looked genuine, I was envious of her. *I
should've won*, I thought to myself, as the two of us stood
side by side while our picture was taken for the yearbook.
While she wore a beautiful crown, I wore a fake smile. At
seventeen years old, I was convinced that I'd lost a once in a
lifetime opportunity to wear a royal crown.

How wrong I was. Years later, when Sarah was a little
girl, she would show me that crowns aren't just for homecoming queens.

On Halloween night, in the autumn of 1991, there was a
blizzard in central Minnesota. That October evening, I
stood near the front door of our entryway, peering through
a window. One-year-old Rachael, our third daughter, was
busy, pulling herself up to a small table that held a bowl
of trick-or-treat candy. I watched as heavy white flakes
covered the candle-lit pumpkins that adorned the porches
of our cul-de-sac.

"Expect ten feet before this is over, folks," the weather-
man proclaimed from the radio in our kitchen.

From where I stood, I kept an eye on my husband as he
trudged through the snow. Flashlight in tow, he guided six-
year-old Sarah and three-year-old T. T. as they rang door-
bells; our neighbors dropping candy into their bags. Sarah,
dressed like a princess in a snowsuit, was trying to steady

her steps in the white drifts, her little pink boots, sopping wet.

As the wind swirled, her tiara blew off her head. T. T., also dressed like a princess, was wearing a spangled crown under a hooded jacket lined with fur. She began crying as her trick-or-treat bag was suddenly whisked into a funnel of whirling white, her candy bars and lollipops dotting the drifts.

It's going to be a long winter, I told myself, as Rachael toppled over the bowl of candy.

That year, from Halloween to Easter, it almost never stopped snowing. With three small children, I hardly ever got out of the house, except to take the kids to the doctor or to buy groceries. I was quarantined. My daily uniform included a pair of sweatpants, an oversized T-shirt, and fur slippers. My hair was always pulled back into a ponytail on top of my head.

I could no longer give Sarah my undivided attention. In a way, that was good. I had stopped defining myself as the mother of a handicapped child. Now, I was just a busy mom. After all the trials we had been through with Sarah, I thought that caring for two able-bodied kids would be a breeze. I was quickly enlightened.

With Don working three nights a week, teaching at a junior college to supplement our income, I was always on duty. One of the kids always needed something—a bottle, a change of clothes, a hug, or two or three. Sometimes I forgot what day of the week it was. There was no distinguishing day hours from night.

I'm always working, I told myself. I'd never been so tired.

Rachael was especially challenging. With her rosy baby cheeks and round hazel eyes, she was fascinated with the way that pencils fit into light sockets. (I quickly childproofed our home.) When I wasn't looking, she would often pull herself up on a chair and fling open the cereal cupboards. She liked munching on Cocoa Puffs and shaking Cheerios all over the floor.

That winter, as Rachael took her first steps, she hobbled around our living room, pulling at lamps, chewing on pillows and tossing decorative tea cups like they were baseballs.

"Mommy...Mommy," she would say, as she reached her chubby arms out to me, hour after hour, her blonde baby strands looking as if she had been through a windstorm. I called her "Wild Thing."

T. T., on the other hand, was a compliant toddler. With freckles dotting her face, she followed me everywhere, her dark eyes always dreamy.

"Mommy, you should comb your hair into pigtails," T. T. would tell me as I stood in front of the bathroom mirror, rushing to get ready each morning before Sarah awoke and Rachael started rattling her crib. Even as a toddler, T. T. was offering me suggestions and affirmations.

"Mom, you can be anything you want to be...Mom, when you grow up, you can even be that good witch on the *Wizard of Oz*," she would say.

It was obvious that Christina and Rachael were developing at a much faster pace than their older sister. Even so, it was comforting to see the relationship between my daughters unfold.

From the very beginning, Christina and Rachael seemed to sense that Sarah needed special attention. Every afternoon, the three of them would watch *Barney*, the dinosaur, on TV. One afternoon, Sarah started singing along with the theme song of the show, slowly stuttering her way through the popular ditty.

All at once, my three daughters were singing along with her, bobbing their heads in time, following Sarah's sluggish lead: "I...I...l-l-l-love...you..., you...l-love...m-m-mmeeee," they sang aloud; their slow-paced voices filled with glee.

Every night as the winter winds rattled outside our windows, the girls and I would cuddle on the couch and read fairy tales. With Rachael on my lap, T. T. sat on one side while Sarah lounged on the other. "Once upon a time, there was a girl named Cinderella," I read one night as I opened to the first page of a tale I knew by heart.

While we paged through the classic story, my daughters marveled at the way Cinderella was gradually transformed from a peasant girl into a stunning princess.

"I...I...I'm a princess, too," Sarah said, as we turned to the last page. She pointed to an illustration of a princess dressed in a glimmering gown and a gilded crown.

I looked at Cinderella, beautifully groomed, looking unquestionably royal.

"I wish I looked like her," I joked to the kids, as I brushed a stray strand of hair from my eyes.

I began thinking about my past, remembering the hopes and dreams of my youth. Memories of my college years began to surface.

In the late 1970s, I had attended an all-women's Catholic college in St. Paul, Minnesota. For young women like myself, it was a decade of transition. The women's movement was gaining momentum. In unprecedented numbers, women were preparing for careers and entering the fields that had been typically held by men. Many of my female classmates were studying to become doctors, lawyers, legislators.

"You can do anything or be anything you want to be," the nuns and professors at my college had said. I was a modern woman of the 70s. I would get my degree. I would teach high school. I would write for magazines. I would secure book contracts. *When I have a family, I'll keep working,* I had told myself at twenty years of age.

After Sarah was born, all my plans changed. It wasn't just Sarah's disability that influenced my decision to become a full-time mother. I simply wanted to be home with my kids. I didn't want to miss all the "firsts" of their childhood: first steps, first laughs, first words.

Still, the vocation of motherhood was humble and hard and most times hidden from the rest of the world. There were no coworkers to eat lunch with, no opportunities to lead classroom discussions, no time to publish magazine articles. There was little praise for the job I was doing.

Sarah studied the illustration of crowned princess, pulling the book up to her face so that she could get a better look. She kept patting my head as if she was looking for something. "Mom…," Sarah said, her eyes beaming with light underneath her glasses. "Y-yyoou are a p-p-princess, even—even—even if you c-c-can't see your crown."

The winter months wore on and Sarah's fascination with fairy tales, especially the story of Cinderella, grew and grew. Soon she began collecting crowns. At first, she just started saving the free cardboard crowns from Burger King. After I started telling my friends and family about Sarah's ongoing intrigue with crowns, my Down syndrome daughter began receiving unexpected gifts. My sister Annie gave Sarah a gold crown rimmed with red hearts. My mother gave her a crown decorated with pink feathers. Don found a plastic crown that was dotted with blue jewels at the Dollar Store. Soon the shelves in Sarah's room were brimming with her toy tiaras, a collection that brought her great pride.

T. T. and Rachael didn't seem to mind that Sarah was receiving so much attention. Sarah was always generous with her crowns. Often the three of them would play together in Sarah's room, trying on crown after crown as they stood in front of a large mirror.

"Rachael...try...try this one. T. T., here is one for you," Sarah would say as she offered tiaras to her sisters.

One afternoon, while I washed clothes in our downstairs laundry room, I heard my three girls playing "dress-up" in an adjacent playroom. I peeked in on them. A trunk filled with my old dresses and blouses was wide open, my outdated clothes tossed and strewn all over the floor.

Sarah was dressed in one of my old nightgowns, a flowered scarf thrown around her shoulders. T. T. wore an oversized bathrobe while Rachael wore nothing but a diaper; she was waving a blinking scepter. "Let the coronation begin," T. T. said, as she began draping a red quilt over a folding chair.

I was glad they were occupied. It gave me a moment to collect my thoughts. As I began putting laundry into the dryer, I heard gusts of wind blowing outside our home.

"Mommy...c-come p-p-play w-with us," Sarah's voice echoed from the playroom.

I continued folding clothes, knowing that I could finish a full load of wash while they played. "I'll be there in a minute," I told them.

As I worked, I turned my glance toward a small plaque that hung above my washing machine. My grandmother "Mema" had given it to me a few years earlier, before she passed away. The sign had once hung in her home, above her sewing machine. It read: A Day Hemmed in Love Rarely Unravels.

An image of Mema's face appeared in my mind's eye; her happy, wrinkled face, her hopeful eyes magnified beneath bifocals. During the hard years of the Depression, Mema had worked at a factory, making metal products from midnight to morning while her five children slept. Like so many families that endured the hardships of the Depression, Mema's family was poor. "In those days, everyone worked hard...families took care of one another," Mema had said.

I thought about the sacrifices Mema had made as a young mother. I imagined her working from dusk to dawn in a noisy factory, trying to stay awake as she assembled small parts of metal.

She must've been so tired, I told myself, as I thought of her coming home in the early morning hours, after a long night of working, to five children and endless household chores. *She worked day and night, without a break,* I told myself.

Then a strange thought occurred to me. *Mema's kids grew up.*

After my grandmother's kids were grown, Mema began her own in-home sewing business, something she had always dreamed of doing. In her basement workshop, Mema's work at her antique sewing machine had brought her great joy and contentment. Most of her customers were family and friends. She loved hemming pants and stitching curtains, pillows, and quilts. "I like working at home, I get to see my family every day," Mema used to say.

Mema worked hard because she loved her family, I thought. My grandmother had done so much with her life. She had been a good mother. She had been a loyal factory worker. In time, she had become a successful businesswoman.

At each stage in her life, Mema had worked hard and loved much, even though her "jobs" were humble and often hidden from the world.

In time, she did everything she wanted to do, I thought.

I stopped folding clothes.

"Mommy, come quick, it's time for the coronation," I heard T. T. call out.

I left my towels in the laundry basket. I made my way to the playroom. There, T. T. and Rachael began dressing me in my old maternity clothes, a plaid-bow blouse and an outdated corduroy jumper.

"Hail to Princess M-mom," Sarah proclaimed, as she led me to the makeshift throne, a folding chair draped with a quilt. Then Sarah placed a Burger King crown on my head.

"To the Queen!" my children chimed as they curtsied in front of me.

"Why, thank you," I replied, as I bowed my head like I was royalty.

The girls giggled with delight.

On another day, I would teach a class or write a book. Today I was doing exactly what I wanted to do. I was being a mom. It was a good day to work hard and love much, a day to "hem in love."

"I wish I could see how I looked," I said, as I adjusted my crown.

Sarah stared at me curiously, her glasses sliding down her nose.

"Mommy," she said, "you're s-s-still a p-p-p-princess... even if you...can't...s-s-s-seeee your crown."

Ponderings

crown (kroun): an ornament for the head, in
the form of a wreath or garland, worn as a sym-
bol of honor, victory, joy, and so on. (New
Webster Encyclopedic Dictionary of the English Language.)

When you look in the mirror, what do you see? Do you
look like a royal child of God? Do you stand tall and proud,
dressed in the finery of God's love and compassion? Do your
eyes shine with the confidence of Christ, like jewels of joy?
Can you see your crown?

Perhaps the challenges of life have veiled the regal reflection that God wants you to see. Maybe your reflection
looks more like that of Cinderella, a spiritually impover-
ished peasant, preoccupied with the responsibilities and
duties of daily life.

If you feel like you are living the life of a servant, the
hours of your days filled with endless tasks and chores, don't
forget that you are part of God's royal kingdom. In Psalm
149, we read, "For the LORD takes delight in his people; he
crowns the humble with salvation…" (v. 4, NIV).

The humble work you do on earth will make a difference if it's done in love. Just think, *Someday you'll arrive in
heaven and God himself will honor you with an eternal crown.*
Until then, work hard, love much…and take Sarah's words
to heart: "You're still a princess [or a prince] even if you
can't see your crown."

SEVEN

Dance in Church

"I t's a mortal sin if you miss Mass," Dad would declare each Sunday morning as he steered our kid-packed station wagon toward our neighborhood church.

Week after week, I sat in the middle of the same wooden pew; my brothers and sisters and parents packed tightly around me. There was no room to move. Dad always sat at the end of the pew, there was more air there—a good place to watch over our family. Often, he would whisper commands and reprimands as needed, his messages traveling from kid to kid. Dad valued order, especially in matters of worship.

Each Sunday, when the opening hymn began, Dad started passing hymnals down our pew. "Open your books…sing," Dad would say. He watched to see if our lips were moving.

When the offertory came, Dad sent the contribution basket down the aisle, waving his hand to make sure we were depositing our church envelopes in a timely manner.

"Keep it moving," Dad commanded. One morning, my little brother, Johnny, forgot his envelope and began digging through his pocket for some loose pennies. "C'mon, get the show on the road," Dad whispered loudly.

At Communion time, Dad always stood at the edge of our pew, inspecting us one by one, making sure our veils and ties were straight before we journeyed down the aisle, hands folded, toward the altar.

Though my father instilled in me a profound reverence and respect for God, I grew up believing that worship was a sacred duty, one that required method, order, and exactness. In Sarah's early years, she showed me that worship could be so much more.

When our three daughters were very young, my husband and I often sat in the back row of church, ready to whisk the children out the door if need be. Sunday after Sunday, while Don held our two youngest in his lap, I kept a watchful eye on Sarah. At the age of nine, Sarah loved church; especially the music. With curly brown hair and thick-lensed glasses, Sarah smiled through each service.

One Sunday, while the organist was playing a lively rendition of "All Creatures of Our God and King," Sarah started tapping her feet. I reached for a hymnal, and in that instant, Sarah slipped into the main aisle of the church. While the entire congregation watched, Sarah made her way to the front and began to dance, twirling and swirling and bowing to the music.

I felt my face flush. "Not again," I whispered to my husband. For the last six Sundays, Sarah had danced in the church aisle when I wasn't looking. As her mother, I felt responsible for the disruption.

"Aw, c'mon, let her dance," my husband said. He thought it was cute.

"Church is for worship," I reminded him firmly. I rushed to retrieve Sarah from the aisle.

Every week as our family sat in the back pew, I prayed: *Lord, please don't let Sarah dance.* God didn't answer my prayer. At the first opportunity, usually during the opening hymn, Sarah would sneak away from me and dance in the aisle, her arms waving like willowy wisps in the wind.

"S-sorry, M-mom…I-I-I couldn't help it," Sarah would stutter as I escorted her back to our pew. "I-I-I love to dance."

In the winter of that year, we enrolled Sarah in first Communion classes that met during Mass on Sunday morning.

"I-I-I'm so excited," Sarah said on the first morning of class. As I guided her to a small desk in the front row of the room, I looked around. All the other children in the room were nondisabled. *I hope no one teases her.*

A teenager with a ponytail drew near. Wearing a tie-dyed shirt and chewing gum, she smiled at my daughter. "Your name is Sarah, isn't it?" the young teacher said, as she knelt down to welcome my little girl with a hug. Our church had made arrangements for an aide to work with Sarah, one-on-one, during the Sunday morning classes. Though I knew my daughter was in good hands, I felt uneasy.

"Sarah likes to dance. She loves music. Sometimes she…"

The teenage girl gave Sarah a high-five. "Cool," she said in her perky adolescent voice. Then she quickly ushered me to the door. "She'll be fine," the girl assured.

After several weeks of preparation, Sarah was finally ready to receive her first Communion. On her big day, our family arrived at church a few minutes early. Sarah was wearing a lace dress with puffed sleeves and a long white veil embroidered with pink roses. With her hair curled into ringlets, she looked like an angel. We took our places in a reserved front row.

Soon the church became crowded and the ushers began

setting up folding chairs. "I hope Sarah doesn't dance today," I whispered to my husband. On this special morning, many nonmembers had come to worship and celebrate.

The organist began playing the opening song and Sarah began swinging her legs to the music.

"Today we welcome our first communicants, the pastor proclaimed from the pulpit. "When I call your name, please come forward to be recognized."

The entire congregation focused on our front row when Sarah's name was called. Making her way toward the pastor, Sarah passed an elderly woman in a wheelchair and came to a halt. The lady smiled at her and Sarah smiled back and curtsied.

Then, as the organ music played on, Sarah made a couple graceful glides and twirled her way toward the pastor, her veil billowing, her face beaming.

I felt my face turn red. I rushed to the aisle to retrieve my child, but as I passed the woman in the wheelchair, she reached out for my hand. "Let her dance! She's just praising God," the woman's eyes sparkled with tears of joy.

I looked around the church. People were grinning from ear to ear. Some were even dabbing their eyes with tissues. I stood in the aisle and watched as Sarah received her certificate from the pastor, and then she twirled her way back to me.

As the congregation applauded, I could hear the voice of God whispering in my heart: *Nancy, Sarah was meant to dance! This is her gift; her special way of worshiping me.*

After the service, I stood in the back of the church, hugging Sarah tightly.

"M-mom...sorry for dancing. I-I-I couldn't help it," she said.

I adjusted her veil so that my husband could take a

picture of her, and I explained that some days were more special than others. "Today, it was okay to dance," I said.

With that, Sarah smiled and bowed like she was onstage.

"Sarah, stop dancing, honey, I've got to take a picture," my husband said, as he checked the flash button on his camera.

I grinned, smugly. "Aw, c'mon," I told him. "Let her dance!"

Ponderings

worship: [from worth] to pay divine honor to, to reverence with respect…to adore. (New Webster Encyclopedic Dictionary of the English Language.)

What does worship mean to you? Is it a Sunday morning routine or a wondrous opportunity to rejoice in God's presence? My daughter Sarah had taught me that worship, in its simplest form, is a celebration of faith and an experience of community that binds lives and hearts.

In Psalm 149, we read: "Let them praise his name with dancing, / making melody to him with tambourine and lyre" (v. 3).

When I reflect on these words, I can't help but think of Sarah, dancing at her first Communion, celebrating God, demonstrating her devotion to a Deity much bigger than herself, a Deity worthy of praise.

The next time you go to church, try following Sarah's lead. Give reverence to God by listening, really listening to the readings and hymns. Swing your feet to the music. Let your eyes sparkle with the light of Christ. Share God's love by looking into the eyes of the people who are seated next to you. Greet them with a handshake or even a hug. Try smiling at them. The grin you offer to a stranger might lift their spirit in a way you cannot comprehend.

Most importantly, don't ever be embarrassed if your soul begins to sing and dance and twirl in church. God loves you. And that's a reason to celebrate.

EIGHT

Sell Free Lemonade

A week before Mother's Day when I was in the sixth grade, I wanted to buy my mom a gift, but I didn't have any money.

I've got an idea, I told myself. I decided to sew her a homemade handkerchief. After cutting a square of fabric from an old pillowcase, I handstitched a piece of red "cast-off" ribbon around the border. Using a needle and red thread, I embroidered misshapen hearts around the edge.

On one corner of the "hanky" I stitched out the word MOM, each letter crookedly sewn, barely readable. It took me days to complete the project. I was so excited when it was finished, I couldn't wait to give it to her. I could barely contain my excitement as I wrapped the gift in a piece of leftover Christmas wrapping; red tissue dotted with white snowflakes.

When Mother's Day arrived, I watched my mom open the gift. I was unprepared for her response. Her eyes welled up with tears. She put her hand over her mouth. She looked at me, shaking her head to and fro.

"It says MOM," I told her, as I pointed to the poorly sewn letters. I thought maybe she couldn't read the word.

"This is the best present," she said, her words slowly

spoken and filled with emotion. She kept looking at the handsewn hanky, wiping away her tears.

I didn't know what to do or say. "Do you like it?" I asked. Mom could only nod. I didn't understand.

It would take years before I would understand. It would take mothering Sarah and her two sisters to comprehend that a gift, given in love, often triggers an unexpected response.

The temperature rose to a muggy ninety-eight degrees on that August afternoon. It was one of those humid, "hard to breathe" days that often define late summer in Minnesota. I stirred a pitcher of lemonade at the kitchen sink. My three little girls sat at the kitchen table, all of them wearing matching sundresses. Rummaging through a box of crayons, they were making a sign on the backside of a wallpaper remnant.

"How do you spell *lemonade*?" Christina asked, as she pulled a thick red marker from the box. She was about five years old; her face tanned and freckled. "L-E-M..." I began sounding out each letter, one by one.

Christina etched the word on the sign while Sarah and Rachael drew hearts and flowers around the border. I looked out the kitchen window. The flowers in our front yard were wilting from the heat. Patches of grass were turning brown. Earlier that morning, I had agreed to let the kids have a lemonade stand. Now, I wondered if it was such a good idea. Our home was air-conditioned, a cool and comfortable refuge from the heat. "It's pretty hot out there," I told the girls, with hesitancy in my voice.

"Mom...it's...it's a g-g-good day," Sarah replied as she

drew a large happy face on one corner of the sign. Her wavy hair was trimmed with yellow barrettes and the frames of her new eyeglasses colored with trendy pink sparkles. Little Rachael just nodded in agreement. While I plunked ice cubes in the pitcher, I listened as my daughters discussed how much to charge for each cup.

"Twenty-five cents," Christina suggested. My middle daughter knew the going rate for lemonade stands. She had often seen her little neighborhood friends selling "quarter-a-cup" Kool-Aid on the corner.

"Three pennies," Rachael countered, as she stood up on her chair and held up four fingers, her pudgy face aglow. She was just learning how to count.

Sarah thought for a moment. Her slanted eyes filled with brightness beneath her glasses. "How... how... how...bout ...f-free?" she suggested.

Though Sarah's Down syndrome was becoming more obvious, marked with ongoing stuttering and a hearing aid, she was an important part of this sisterly trio. Disability or not, T. T. and Rachael respected their sister. She was and would always be the "oldest."

"Freeeeee...," my daughters squealed with delight, their small voices unified. It was clear that Sarah's idea held great possibility.

"We'll be the first ones ever to sell free lemonade," T. T. suggested. I helped the girls print out the word "FREE" in bold marker on the bottom of the sign.

Minutes later, the kids and I made our way to a patch of shade in our front yard where I set up a small table beneath an oak tree. While I helped Sarah tape the sign to the table, T. T. and Rachael set the makeshift stand with rows of paper cups, a soup ladle, and two pitchers of lemonade.

I wish they were doing this on a cooler day, I told myself, as I started watering nearby flowers with the hose.

Soon their first customer, our mailman, approached the stand. Weary from the heat, he set his heavy mailbag down on the grass, wiping the sweat from his brow. "Free lemonade. What could be better?" he replied, as the girls took turns ladling lemonade, serving him five cups in all.

Sarah smiled at him. "It's…a…g-g-goodd d-d-day," she told him.

He patted her on the head. Then he reached into his pocket and handed each of my girls a quarter. "You've made my day," he told the girls, waving at them as he went on his way.

Soon, a twentysomething couple biked to the stand. They parked their mountain bikes in front of our home, both of them looking like competitive athletes. Dressed in bright shorts and T-shirts logoed with the word "Adidas," they were out of breath from pedaling in the sultry summer air.

"The lemonade is free?" the ponytailed girl asked, huffing and puffing with each breath she took. Both of the bikers were sunburned.

"It is…," my girls shouted as they pointed to their sign. The young couple couldn't stop grinning as the kids passed them cup after cup of free lemonade. Just before they biked away, the ponytailed girl reached into a small zippered bag that was strapped to her waist.

"We were so thirsty…you and your sisters deserve this," she said and handed Sarah a five-dollar bill.

"Hoooray…Yay…Weeee," the girls cried out, as they danced around their stand. Sarah waved the bill high so that I could see it.

"You've got another customer," I told them as a white

Mercedes drove up to their stand. While I trimmed bushes, I saw a tall, distinguished looking man get out of his car. He was dressed in a pinstriped suit, a burgundy tie, and sunglasses.

"How much?" he asked, as he pulled his wallet from his pocket. He didn't even look at the kids. His brow was furrowed. He looked preoccupied with the business concerns of his day.

Sarah drew near to him. She looked up at him, her pink glasses shining in the sun. He took off his sunglasses and made eye contact with Sarah.

"It's….it's…it's…f-free," Sarah said.

The man gazed at my children, his eyes moving from child to child. In an instant, his stern face melted into tenderness. "Free?" he asked, his eyes beginning to mist. The girls gave him four cups of lemonade and "threw in" one cup "to go."

"Here, buy something for yourselves," he said, as he handed each of the kids a $10 bill.

The rest of the afternoon as I did yard work, the kids served free lemonade to all who passed by, mothers pushing canopied strollers, men toting golf clubs, workers in cars and trucks and vans.

While customers kept giving the girls dimes and quarters and multiple bills, I found myself rushing back and forth from the house tucking their "donations" into a coffee mug while I refilled pitchers of ice-cold lemonade.

We finally ran out of lemonade at 4:00 in the afternoon. After closing down the stand, the girls and I gathered, once more, in our air-conditioned kitchen. While they sat at the table, I helped them count up their coins and bills, the "earnings" they had never expected to receive.

"Sixty-two dollars and twenty-six cents," I said, as Rachael began playing with a pile of pennies. T. T. quickly wrote down the total on a Post-it note.

"We'll always remember this day," T. T. said, as she proudly attached the note to the fridge with a magnet shaped like a frog.

"M-mommy...it...it...was a g-g-good day," Sarah said, hugging me.

On one of the hottest days of the summer, Sarah had given us a great "idea." She had presented us with an opportunity, a chance to give away love, freely, without measure, condition, or charge. She had shown us how to offer "cups of compassion," how to sell "free lemonade," how to experience the joy of generosity without expecting anything in return.

As Sarah and her sisters ladled kindness into paper cups, their charity was recognized and rewarded. Even so, their monetary blessing would never compare with the laughter and love they shared that afternoon. It had been a good day. They had served others. That in itself was their true reward.

"How would you like to spend the money?" I asked the kids.

T. T. wanted to go out for ice cream. Rachael wanted to get French fries at McDonald's. "Let's...let's...let's buy more lemonade," Sarah suggested.

Once again, Sarah had a great idea. There was plenty of money to buy all three.

Ponderings

give, giv: *to convey to another, to bestow, to grant.* (New Webster Encyclopedic Dictionary of the English Language.)

Think about how many opportunities you have each day to give—simply give. You can smile at a crabby neighbor. You can let an elderly person take your " spot" in the grocery checkout line. You can write a card of encouragement. You can visit a lonely "shut in." You can donate to a worthy cause.

Sometimes it's the smallest acts of kindness that can make the biggest difference. Jesus tells us that humble gestures of charity, shared freely and without condition, will be remembered and recognized in heaven. In Matthew 10:42 we read:

> *Whoever gives even a cup of cold water to one of*
> *these little ones in the name of a disciple—truly*
> *I tell you, none of these will lose their reward.*

Sarah has taught me that "giving," just for the sake of giving, is a beautiful way to experience the "rewards of heaven," right here on earth. It really is "fun" to give to others, to bestow joy, to impart tenderness, to grant someone, unexpectedly, the measureless gifts of faith, hope, and love.

Today, be like Sarah. Make some eye contact with people who pass by the lemonade stand of your life. Smile at them. Start pouring your own "cups of compassion." Sell free lemonade. Give. There's no telling what might happen.

(From left to right) Rachael, Christina (T. T.), and Sarah

NINE

Try New Things

J ean Nelson lived on Ivy Lane at the end of a tree-lined road, in a small vine-covered cottage that overlooked a winding creek. In the summertime when I was young, my mother, five sisters, and I would visit Jean every Wednesday morning. Jean lived about a mile from our home.

I remember one sunlit morning when Mom drove our station wagon into Jean's gravel driveway, steering our car right up to the sun porch that lined the front of her house. From the back seat where I sat, I could see Jean waiting for us, sitting in her wheelchair, smiling at us through the screen.

"Mag, you're here…and you brought the girls," Jean proclaimed as she called out my mother's nickname and we all tumbled through the door of the porch. Like always, my sisters and I took turns giving her hugs. Though Jean had limited use of her hands, and hugging was hard, her bright countenance was welcome enough.

My mother had known Jean since high school. As a child, I had heard stories of their enduring friendship. When they were in their late teens, Jean and Mom had worked as secretaries in downtown law offices that were just a few blocks apart. During those years, Jean and Mom were young, attractive, and single. They met for lunch and noontime shopping

sprees, often double-dating. I'd seen photos of them walking arm in arm, outside downtown stores, the two of them
wearing trendy business suits and brimmed hats. They had
remained close throughout the years, although my mother's
life had turned out much differently than Jean's.

"Mag" had married my father in her early twenties. The
seasons of my mother's life had been filled with the joys and
challenges of being married, raising nine children, and keeping up a home.

Jean, on the other hand, was confined to a wheelchair
by the time she was twenty-five; diagnosed with multiple
sclerosis, paralyzed from the waist down. She never got married or had a family. Instead, Jean had lived on Ivy Lane for
decades, her devoted mother tending to her special needs.

"You girls get prettier every time I see you," Jean said, as
she shook her head, dramatizing amazement as she studied
each of our faces to determine which one of us looked most
like "Mag." Soon Jean's mother, frail and wrinkled, came
out from the kitchen holding a china teapot. A sweet, fruity
fragrance filled the sun porch as Jean's mother began pouring strawberry-scented tea into two porcelain cups with wide
handles; one for my mother and one for Jean.

While Mom and Jean sat on the sun porch chatting and
sipping tea, my sisters and I played outside, running through
the green land that blanketed Jean's backyard. We picked
flowers and played croquet. We took turns tossing pebbles
into water.

About noontime, as I waded in the creek, I watched my
mother guide Jean's wheelchair from the sun porch, over
the grass, and down toward the water. While my mother
lounged on the grass, Jean sat by her side; the steel frame of
her wheelchair reflecting rays of sunlight.

I didn't hear what they were saying, but I could see them laughing, talking, nodding their heads. I stared at them for several seconds at a time. I couldn't look away. Even though I was very young, I knew that I was viewing something rare and all-together lovely. I hoped that one day I would know a friendship as true as theirs.

On that long-ago summer morning, I began learning a basic truth about life, one that my daughter Sarah has re-taught me over and over again. It's a privilege to look at loveliness.

I steered my grocery cart through the aisle, sifting through coupons and checking off items on my weekly "food list." Rachael and T. T., both toddlers, sat in the main part of the cart, cheerfully organizing the food I tossed in the basket; boxes of cereal, bunches of broccoli, cartons of eggs and milk. Looking back now, it's hard to believe that T. T. and Rachael were once so small. During those years, their little legs and arms were a perfect fit for a grocery cart.

On that Monday afternoon, Sarah sat in the upper cart, in the child seat, swinging her legs. That was her special place. There she could get a better look at the colorful pack-ages of food and she could practice pronouncing three-syl-labled words such as cauliflower or cinnamon.

"Mommm...you...you...should t-t-try new t-t-things," Sarah said, as she pointed to a shelf where jumbo bottles of mango juice were displayed. I nodded, but I was preoccu-pied, searching for a coupon. Sarah took advantage of the moment. Turning her glance toward an opposite shelf, she scooped up a bag of beef jerky, pitching it into the cart.

"Sarah, no...we don't need that," Rachael and T. T. declared, their little voices echoing through the store. Sarah grinned, her slanted eyes beaming with mischief, her smile defying the droopy muscles around her mouth.

I shook my head in dismay. "Sarah, you can't keep doing this," I said with a sigh. I retrieved the bag of jerky from the cart and placed it in her hand. "You need to put this back," I told her.

Going to the grocery store was a sensory experience for Sarah. At six years old, she had mastered the art of leaning over the cart, just far enough so that her hands could "feel" the rough peeling of a cantaloupe or the softness of cotton balls in a bag. Inevitably when I wasn't looking, Sarah would sneak something into our cart, something we didn't need.

Week after week, people would stare at Sarah as she pulled exotic items from the shelves; tins of sardines, bottles of red sherry, cans of anchovies. That afternoon, as I helped Sarah put the jerky back into place, a well-groomed woman in her late fifties strolled past; her cart neatly arranged with bottled water, deli meat, and bread from the bakery. Wearing a dark pantsuit and gold necklace, the woman stopped and stared at Sarah, studying her face for several seconds.

Whenever I took the girls out in public, to the post office, the drug store, the bank, people stared. They stared at Sarah. They stared at me. They stared at my other children. I had ignored the glances and glares of strangers long enough. That afternoon, as I stood in that grocery aisle, I did something I've never done before. I stared back. With my arms crossed over my chest, I looked at the lady in the pantsuit in the same way she looked at Sarah. I mimicked her facial expression, widening my eyes and raising my eyebrows, my glance glued.

I wanted to confront her rudeness. I wanted to say, *Haven't you ever seen a child with disabilities? Didn't anyone teach you that staring is cruel? What ARE you looking at?*

I didn't need to say a word. The sternness in my eyes spoke volumes. I had proclaimed war in the grocery store.

"I'm sorry," the well-groomed woman whispered. She hung her head like a scolded child.

I watched as she strolled away with her shopping cart, my emotions mixed. *I have a right to be angry…it's mean to stare at a disabled child,* I rationalized.

Still, I couldn't get over how remorseful the woman had been. She wasn't an inherently evil person. *I shouldn't have been that hard on her.*

"Mommy, why does everyone look at Sarah?" T. T. asked, as I rolled our cart toward the checkout line. Little Rachael looked up from the cart, waiting for my reply, her hair combed into uneven pigtails, her wide eyes full of innocence.

Sarah just swung her legs to and fro, her thick-lensed glasses reflecting the brightness of her eyes. She was the lucky one. She was completely oblivious to the sea of eyes always watching her, always watching our family. It was T. T. and Rachael who were just beginning to notice that their Down syndrome sister was a public attraction.

"I don't know," I told my two nondisabled daughters. I was at a loss for words, unable to offer them an explanation. I felt empty. *No one understands,* I thought.

That night, I called my sister Annie. "Why do people stare at Sarah?" I asked her. I wanted to have a long conversation with Annie, but she was distracted. She was busy preparing for her wedding, writing out invitations.

"I stare sometimes," Annie replied, as I heard another

phone call beeping in on her telephone line. Just before she hung up, she told me, "Nancy...staring isn't always what it seems." I didn't know what she meant.

The weeks passed and grocery shopping became a dreaded chore. Each Monday, while the kids rode in my cart, I would tell myself, *Don't look at anyone.* While I steered our basket down the food aisles, dodging shoppers with wide turns, I avoided looking at people—at faces. I didn't want to know who was staring.

"Mommy, you look sad," T. T. said one Monday afternoon as I plopped cans of soup and boxes of Hamburger Helper into our cart. Rachael quietly nodded her head as she arranged the cans of mushroom soup.

Sarah waved her palm in front of my face, trying to make eye contact with me as she sat in the upper cart.

"Mommmmy, you...you...you...s-s-should t-t-try something new," she said, her eyeglasses slipping down her nose, as she pointed to a giant box of Jujubes. I feigned a smile. The girls knew that something wasn't quite right.

The following Sunday morning, while Don watched the kids, I got up early and went to 7:30 Mass at our local church. I arrived late, about fifteen minutes after the Mass started, right before the Gospel reading.

I didn't want to call attention to my untimely arrival, so I quietly made my way to the family room, a windowed room that overlooked the main church; a worship space lined with folding chairs and toy-filled shelves.

My husband and I had spent many Sundays in the family room, usually during the 10:30 Mass. It was a comfortable place to care for our little ones while watching the church service through the windows. The family room always got crowded during the later morning Masses; it was soundproof refuge for young parents, crying babies, and toddlers having temper tantrums.

However, on this Sunday morning when I opened the door to the family room, I was surprised that it was empty. *Everyone is still sleeping,* I told myself.

I took a seat by the window. I looked at the sparse congregation that sat in the pews beyond the panes; an early morning crowd, mostly elderly. It was peaceful. I closed my eyes while a voice clattered through the loudspeaker on the wall. It was the voice of a male lector standing at the altar, announcing the responsorial psalm: "If today you hear God's voice, harden not your heart…" came the staticky words, a radio-like message that sounded like an old record playing on a broken phonograph.

The congregation began singing as the door of the family room opened. I watched as a tall, middle-aged man with broad shoulders propped open the door, holding it in place with one foot. He looked like a seasoned football coach. With a tan face and a strong chin, he wore a red nylon jacket and a baseball cap.

He was with a young teenager, a dark-haired boy in a wheelchair. The man struggled to keep open the door while trying to maneuver the cumbersome wheelchair through the door.

"Here, let me help you," I told him. I sprung from my seat to hold the door in place.

The man looked at me, his eyes full of kindness. "These wheelchairs…sometimes they have a mind of their own," he said jokingly. I smiled.

The baseball-capped man took a place a few feet away from me, rolling the wheelchair to his side.

"Our offertory hymn can be found on page 154…" came

a rattling voice through the speakers. From the corner of my eye, I glanced at the youth. Dressed in a maroon letter jacket from a local high school, he looked about sixteen years old. He wore blue jeans and running shoes.

In most every way, he looked like a normal teenager, except for his eyes. His eyes were dazed, deep brown, and unfocused. I wondered if he'd been in an accident.

Don't stare at him…it's mean, I told myself. I reached for two songbooks on a nearby shelf, right above a small playhouse. I handed one of the hymnals to the middle-aged man.

Soon, a beautiful baritone voice began filling the room as the man began singing, his soul-stirring song rising above the organ music that clanked through the wall speakers.

"Oh, God, our help in ages past, a shelter from the storm…," he sang with one arm around the shoulder of his disabled son.

I peeked over my songbook. The boy was rocking back and forth, his gaze distant.

I wonder if he had a brain injury…I wonder if they are father and son…I bet this has been hard on his family, I thought. I was curious. Once more, I caught myself looking at them. *Don't stare…,* I thought. I had to force myself to turn away.

When Communion time came, the door of the family room opened. Our priest, dressed in a dark robe and white collar, drew near to us. Carrying a gold plate brimming with white Hosts, the sacramental bread of our faith, the priest began tracing a small cross on the forehead of the disabled boy.

"Body of Christ," the priest whispered as he handed the man one of the Hosts. I couldn't help but notice what happened next. The baseball-capped man reverently broke the Host into two equal pieces.

"This is Jesus," the man told the boy in the wheelchair. With the unmistakable tenderness of a loving parent, he placed the Host in the mouth of the handicapped boy, waiting patiently until he swallowed it.

I tried to look away, but I couldn't. I was viewing something that beckoned to me to "look," to stand in wonder. It was like I was witnessing something akin to a glorious sunset streaming down from heaven, its rays tinging the earth with colorful hues.

I had never witnessed such devotion. Clearly this child was handicapped, weak, and unresponsive, completely dependent on others in every conceivable way. In contrast, the man who accompanied him was a vision of self-sufficiency, and yet, a selfless giver of care.

This is the meaning of unconditional love, I thought. I didn't know them. They didn't know me. Yet, as I watched them, I was blessed.

I'm glad I'm here...to see this, I told myself, as the priest drew near to my chair and placed a Host in my hand.

"Body of Christ," the priest said.

"Amen," I replied. I closed my eyes, pausing for a moment of quiet prayer. An image of Sarah's Down syndrome face surfaced in my mind's eye. I thought about countless stares she endured simply because she was disabled.

As Sarah's mother, I had grown defensive and hard-hearted, wrongly assuming that every stare was a rude glance, an intrusive glimpse, a cruel glare. Now, as I sat in the family room "looking" at these two very precious strangers, I wondered if there might be other reasons why people watched my Down syndrome daughter.

Maybe Sarah blesses people...the way I've been blessed this morning, I told myself. I remembered the well-groomed woman in the grocery store. I'd been angry at her, simply because she "looked" at Sarah. I had treated her like an enemy, without even knowing who she was or what she was thinking. Now, I was pondering my encounter with her in a whole new way.

Maybe she was curious…maybe she wondered why Sarah had slanted eyes. Maybe she noticed that Sarah was a precious member of our family, that we loved her, despite her obvious handicaps and limitations.

"Our closing hymn is 'Amazing Grace,'" a tinny voice clattered from the speaker box.

I listened as the man sang the words I had once memorized as a child: "Through many dangers, toils and snares, I have already come…'Twas grace that brought me safe thus far, and grace will lead me home…."

As the organist played the final verse of the song, the man began wheeling his young companion toward the door. I held it open for them.

"Don't you just love the family room?" the man joked as the last note of the organ vibrated through the wall speakers like a spoon clanging in a tin can.

I laughed. "Those speakers really add that 'special touch,'" I replied.

He tipped his baseball cap. "Have a great day," he said.

The following afternoon, like every Monday afternoon, I took the girls grocery shopping. I steered my kid-packed cart down the food aisles, holding my food list and sifting through coupons. As usual, people stared. They stared at Sarah. They stared at me. They stared at my children.

I didn't feel defensive. I looked them in the eye, nodding to them, acknowledging their presence with an accepting smile. I didn't know who they were or what they were thinking—but God did. It was okay that they looked. I could trust that God was capable of using Sarah's disability to teach them, to bless them, to remind them, that "weakness" doesn't make a person unlovable. When the right time came, I would share these newly gained insights with T. T. and Rachael. I would tell them that "staring" isn't always what it seems.

"Mommy, you look happy," T. T. said, as I pulled a box of Lucky Charms from the shelf. Little Rachael nodded as she arranged cartons of milk.

Just then, an elderly man shuffled past, his gait sluggish and slow. He took time to stop, to look at my kids, to pat Sarah on top of the head. "You have beautiful children," he told me, waving good-bye as he made his way toward the juice aisle.

"Mommy...you...you...should...t-try...n-n-new...t-things," Sarah said, as she leaned over the cart, scooping up a package of mouse traps, flinging them into the cart.

"Sarah...put that back...we don't need those," T. T. and Rachael called out, their little voices rising through the aisle.

I took the mousetrap into my hands. "You never know, I might need these someday," I told the girls. Rachael and T. T. laughed as they looked at the traps. From her upper perch in the cart, Sarah swung her legs to and fro, smiling smugly.

My Down syndrome daughter was right. I needed to think new thoughts. I needed to try new things.

Ponderings

*look (luk): to direct the eye toward an object,
to gaze, to consider.* (New Webster Encyclopedic Dictionary of the English Language.)

Life is filled with the sights and images that beckon us to
"look." Just this morning as I jogged through our neighborhood, I noticed that the roses in my neighbor's garden were
just beginning to bloom. I stopped. I couldn't turn my eyes
away from the beauty of the salmon-colored blossoms.

While roses are wondrous to behold, there is a beauty
that isn't so obvious. It's the understated loveliness that ra-
diates from the face of a handicapped person, dependent in
so many ways, yet completely sufficient in the grace of God.
It's the unelaborated beauty that shines from the eyes and
hearts of countless caregivers, those who tend to the weak-
est among us, in the quiet and humble ways, without any
need or want of recognition.

The handicapped are God's special people. I think many
of the disabled are "angels on a mission" sent to teach the
world lessons of humility and hope. God watches over them.
He "considers" them. He turns his eyes upon them.

In Psalm 138, we read these simple but poignant words:
"Though the LORD is high, he regards the lowly" (v. 6).

The next time you see a handicapped person and their
companions, take a moment to pray for them. Offer a warm
glance of acceptance. Let your expression convey respect and
graciousness. Look at them the way God does. With love.

TEN

Be a Good Friend

The walls of my teenage room were decorated with trendy posters from the 1970s. My little sister, Annie, loved my room. Every afternoon, while I did homework at my desk, Annie would flop on my bed, gazing dreamily at the colorful pictures and prints that were taped from floor to ceiling.

One afternoon, toward the end of my senior year, Annie lay on my bed, reading aloud the verses that trimmed each poster: If you love something, let it go... Make peace, not war... Smile, God loves you...

I was annoyed. "Annie, don't you have something better to do?" I said, as I looked up from my book.

My little sister drew near and looked at me with wide curious eyes. "But you're my best friend," she said.

On the night that I graduated from high school, Annie came into my room and handed me a homemade gift, a "poster" she had made from a paper bag and colored markers. She had drawn two oversized hands reaching out to each other. Beneath the outstretched hands was a caption that read: TOGETHERNESS IS ENDLESS.

"That's us," Annie said, as she pointed to the misshapened hands.

"This is very nice," I told her. I was touched. The makeshift poster was Annie's way of saying: "You will always be my sister...our friendship will last forever."

I still have Annie's poster. Though it's yellow with age, I can't bear to throw it out. Annie taught me that a true bond of friendship endures all things. So did Sarah.

I pulled the pink envelope from our mailbox just as my daughter was coming home from school. It looked like a birthday party invitation. "SARAH" was carefully printed in bold, black letters. When Sarah stepped off the bus I tucked the envelope into her hand. "It's...it's...for me," she stuttered, delighted.

In the unseasonably warm February sun we sat down on the front porch. As I helped her open the envelope, I wondered who had sent it. Maybe Emily or perhaps Michael; pals from her special-education class.

"It's...it's...from Maranda!" Sarah said, pointing to the front of the card. There, framed with hearts, was a photo of a girl I had never seen before. She had beautiful long hair, a dimpled grin, and warm smiling eyes. "Maranda is eight years old," the caption read. "Come and celebrate on Valentine Day."

Glancing at the picture, I felt uneasy. Clearly, Maranda was not handicapped. Sarah, on the other hand, was still functioning on a preschool level. At age nine, she was just beginning to write letters and a few words.

My daughter had many friends who used wheelchairs and braces, but this was the first time she had been invited to the home of a nondisabled child. "How did you meet Maranda?" I asked.

"At...at...school. We eat lunch together every...every day."

Even though Sarah was in special education, she socialized with other second- and third-graders during gym, lunch, and homeroom. I had always hoped she would make friends outside her program. Why, then, did I feel apprehensive?

Because I'm her mother, I thought. I couldn't help but feel protective of Sarah. I knew a friendship with Sarah would call for extra sensitivity, tolerance, and understanding. Was the child in the photo capable of that?

Valentine Day came. Sarah dressed in her favorite pink lace dress and white patent leather shoes. As we drove to Maranda's party, she sat next to me in the front seat, clutching the Barbie doll she had wrapped with Winnie-the-Pooh paper and masking tape. "I...I'm so excited," she said.

I smiled, but deep inside I felt hesitant. There would be other children at the party. Would they tease Sarah? Would Maranda be embarrassed in front of her other friends?

Don't let Sarah get hurt, I prayed.

I pulled into the driveway of a house decorated with silver heart-shaped balloons. Waiting at the front door was a little girl in a red sweater trimmed with ribboned hearts. It was Maranda. "Sarah's here!" she called. Racing to our car, she welcomed my daughter with a wraparound hug. Soon seven giggling girls followed Maranda's lead, welcoming Sarah with smiles.

"Bye, Mom," Sarah said, waving as she and the others ran laughing into the house. Maranda's mother, Mary, greeted me at my rolled-down car window.

"Thanks for bringing Sarah," she said. "Maranda is so excited Sarah could come to her party." Mary went on to explain that her daughter was an only child and that Maranda and Sarah had become special friends at school. "Maranda talks about her all the time," she said.

I drove away, amazed at the way Sarah had been welcomed. Still, I couldn't get over my uneasiness. Could this friendship ever be equal? Maranda would need to learn the language of Sarah's speech. She would need patience when Sarah struggled with certain tasks. That was a lot to ask of an eight-year-old.

As the months passed I watched the girls' friendship grow. They spent many hours together in our home. Fixing dinner in the kitchen, I often heard giggles fill the family room as they twirled around an old recliner or watched *The Lion King*. Sometimes they dressed up in my old hats and outdated blouses, pretending to be famous singers.

When the school year came to a close, Sarah and Maranda spent the summer months playing together in our backyard, running through the sprinkler and playing hide-and-seek.

The following autumn, as the leaves fell outside our home, Sarah and Maranda sat together each afternoon at our kitchen table. Sarah held a pencil. Maranda had a tablet of paper.

Maranda called out each letter as she guided Sarah's hand, "S-A-R-A-H." Though some of the letters had been printed backward or upside-down, Maranda praised Sarah's effort. "Great job," she said, applauding.

Their friendship continued to grow. At Christmastime the girls exchanged gifts. Sarah gave Maranda a photograph of herself, a framed first Communion picture.

"You look beautiful," Maranda said, as she admired Sarah's white ruffled dress and long lace veil. In return, Maranda gave Sarah a gray-flannel elephant trimmed with an "I love you" tag. It quickly became Sarah's favorite stuffed animal, and she slept with it every night.

Then a few weeks into the new year, Sarah came home from school looking downcast. "M-Maranda is...is sick," she said. I thought maybe she had caught the bug circulating at school. Minutes later, however, Sarah's special-education teacher called. Maranda was in the hospital. She had sustained a seizure at school and had been diagnosed with a brain tumor. Surgeons had performed a risky operation, which had left Maranda paralyzed on one side with impaired speech and vision. The biopsy results weren't back yet.

"Can we visit her?" I asked. I knew Sarah would want to see her friend.

"Maranda is very despondent and not up to seeing anybody," the teacher told me. "Her parents are requesting cards rather than visits."

"We'll keep her in our prayers," I promised.

That night Sarah knelt beside her bed, clutching her stuffed elephant. "Please ma-ma make Maranda better," she prayed. Night after night she implored God to heal her friend. Then one night in early February Sarah stopped abruptly in the middle of her prayer. She nudged me.

"Let's ma...ma...make a valentine for Ma...Maranda."

The next day we sat together at the kitchen table as I helped Sarah write Maranda's name on a large sheet of pink-and-white construction paper. She decorated each letter with stickers and glittery markers. She drew a large heart around the name, and then glued candy hearts with phrases like "friends forever" and "be mine." In similar fashion she added four more pages. Just before we slid the card into a large envelope, Sarah asked, "How...how...how do I spell love?"

I called out the letters as she painstakingly printed

"LOVE," the letters crooked and out of place. Then she signed her name.

Two weeks passed. We heard that Maranda had additional surgery. On Valentine Day I got a phone call from her mother. "Maranda's home," she said, "and wants to see Sarah."

"Home?" I asked with surprise.

"Maranda's tumor was benign. We're hoping for a full recovery."

While we discussed her prognosis, Maranda's mom relayed how thankful she was for Sarah and her card. "Maranda was very depressed. She had stacks of letters, cards and gifts, but wouldn't open any of them. Then one morning Sarah's homemade card arrived. We opened it and Maranda burst into a huge smile. She hugged it and wouldn't put it down." Mary's voice was choked with emotion. "It was an answer to our prayers."

I hung up the phone and realized then that Sarah and Maranda were the truest of friends. Their bond was defined not by intellect or health or handicap, but by love, unconditionally given and received. They had overcome disability with laughter and support. Their friendship had always been equal.

Within a few months, Maranda recovered completely from her illness. Now that her friend was on the mend, Sarah invited Maranda to our home for a sleepover.

As the girls sat at our kitchen table, they talked about Maranda's newly pierced ears and Sarah's "secret" boyfriend from her special-education class. Then in the middle of their conversation Sarah opened a kitchen drawer and pulled out a tablet and pencil.

"S-A-R-A-H," Maranda called out as she had so many times before. Sarah printed her name without any help as

Maranda looked on and clapped. "Great job, Sarah!" she said. I took a peek at my daughter's masterpiece. Her name had been written perfectly.

Ponderings

friend: to love...one who is attached to another by affection, one who has esteem and regard for one another. (New Webster Encyclopedic Dictionary of the English Language.)

Who do you call "friend"? Who do you hold in high esteem? Who do you love?

When I think of my truest friends, I immediately recall the people who supported my husband and I through the first difficult weeks of Sarah's life.

I remember my sisters; they called most every day. I think of the loved ones who stopped by to offer a carefully written card or a hug of encouragement. I think of the many neighbors who made homemade dinners so that we wouldn't have to cook. At one point, we had so many foil-wrapped casseroles that my husband started packing them in the snow banks that lined our sidewalk.

If you have even one true friend, you are blessed indeed. A faithful friend will always stay close, their presence will be a consolation in times of trial. In Proverbs 18:24, we read these words: "Some friends play at friendship / but a true friend sticks closer than one's nearest kin."

Today, do something special for a friend. Call them, just to say hello. Make them a homemade casserole. Be like Sarah. Send them a homemade card and sign it with love.

A recent family vacation to Oregon:
Christina, Nancy Jo, Sarah, and Don, (kneeling) Rachael.

ELEVEN

Face Your Fears

I remember the first time I felt scared, really scared. It was back in the early sixties on a windy afternoon in late August. At five years old, I stood with my father on a high observation deck that overlooked the rocky shoreline of Lake Superior. At that time, our family lived in Duluth, within walking distance of that great and mighty lake.

With the hood of my jacket tied around my face, I watched as Dad hoisted my three sisters (back then we were all so little) onto a secure enclosure that wrapped around the deck, a safe concrete barrier topped with a sitting ledge and a screen. I backed away from the ledge, the winds of late summer biting my nose. I was too short to see over the concrete gate, but I knew we were several feet above the lake. I could smell the moistness of the water and hear the loud lapping of the waves.

"It's too high," I told my father, as he motioned me to the wall. I didn't want to see what was beyond the deck.

"It's safe. You won't fall," Dad said, reassuringly.

My sisters waved to me from the ledge. "C'mon, Nancy, it's fun."

Dad took me in his arms and lifted me up. I peeked over the barrier. I saw the waves whirling, swirling, foaming like soap as they slapped against the black, jagged stones below.

"I can't look!" I cried out. I was frightened. I wanted to go home. I buried my head in my dad's shoulder. That afternoon, I developed a fear of heights that followed me through my growing-up years and well into my adulthood.

By the time I became Sarah's mother, I had convinced myself that the best way to deal with my fear was to avoid elevators, high-rise buildings, and restaurants. My dread of high places was unacceptable to Sarah. During her growing-up years, Sarah helped me face my fears.

I sat on the edge of Sarah's bed in the shadows of evening, a night-light glowing from an outlet by her dresser.

"I'm s-s-scared," she said, as she pulled a pink-checked quilt over her head. Sarah was about ten years old, and we had just moved to a new home. Though I had wallpapered her new room with a cheerful pattern of teddy bears and polka dots, she was still having a hard time adjusting to an unfamiliar place.

"Sarah, you've got to face your fears," I said. I had been reading a book on parenting that suggested children needed to confront their insecurities.

"If your child is afraid, give them a way to deal with it," the author had suggested.

I gently tugged at Sarah's blankets, uncovering her sweet Down syndrome face. I pointed to the night-light, a bright beacon, a small plastic princess beaming from the wall.

"Look…it never stops shining, even in the dark," I said.

Sarah turned her glance toward the glowing princess. "It's…nice," Sarah said. Then, just like that, she dozed off.

After that night, Sarah never feared the dark again. As

the weeks and months passed, Sarah continued to make a smooth transition to her new home, school, and neighborhood. Soon I enrolled her in weekly swimming classes at a local community center. Since Sarah was the only non-disabled child in a class of ten children, she was assigned an aide, a young college girl named Mary who was studying to be a special-education teacher.

On the first afternoon of class, I stood by the pool, holding Sarah's hand as Mary drew near. Even though I had bought Sarah a new swimsuit, a hot-pink suit patterned with yellow smiley faces, I felt hesitant.

"Sarah might be afraid of the water," I told the aide.

Sarah shook her head defiantly. "M-M-Mom...I'm... not...s-scared," she said, as she stomped her bare feet on the tiled floor.

While the other children began jumping into the pool, Sarah wiggled away from me, following the other young swimmers as she edged her way closer to the water.

"C'mon Sarah, we'll show your mother what you can do," Mary suggested as she reached out for Sarah's hand. Wearing a Speedo bathing suit and a waterproof clip in her dark hair, it was clear that Mary was ready to teach my disabled daughter how to swim. The two of them turned their back on me and leapt into the pool.

Week after week, as Sarah took swimming lessons, I kept a vigil from the bleachers. With young Rachael and T. T. sitting next to me, we clapped and cheered as Sarah splashed across the shallow waters, clutching a foam board. Her orange life preserver shimmered as brightly as her water-drenched smile. Mary always kept a watchful eye on Sarah, guiding my daughter as she learned to kick, splash, and tread.

One afternoon I watched Sarah inch her way across the diving board.

"C'mon, Sarah. Jump. I'll catch you," Mary shouted as she tread water beneath the board, her arms outstretched to my grinning daughter.

"Sarah…wait…," I cried out from my poolside perch. I panicked. Sarah wasn't like other children. She was disabled. "It's too high for Sarah. She'll get scared!" I shouted to Mary, my maternal message echoing across the pool.

Deep inside, I knew I was transferring my own fears onto Sarah. I had been afraid of heights since childhood. Now that I was a grown woman, I still hadn't dealt with my paranoia of high places. Even though Sarah was very young, she and her sisters had already seen me avoid countless elevators whenever I took them to the doctor's office, the mall, or the community center.

Now, as I watched my daughter from the bleachers, I wanted to rescue her from the high heights above the water. But Sarah kept taking fearless steps across the board. Rachael and T. T. looked on, with wide eyes, as their sister blatantly opposed me, disregarding my concerns with a wave of her hand.

"But Mommy, Sarah wants to jump," T. T. said, as she tugged at the hem of my oversized sweatshirt.

Seconds later, Sarah jumped. Her little body sprung from the board, into the pool, right into Mary's waiting arms. A fountain of water spouted upward as her orange life preserver pillowed into the waves.

Mary and Sarah splashed in the water, laughing with glee as they gripped each other's hands.

"See, Mommy. Sarah jumped," T. T. cried out. Rachael waved jubilantly. I breathed a sigh of relief while Sarah giggled, gulping water with every wave of her hand.

Sarah grew and so did her fearlessness. Often when she played with T. T. and Rachael in the backyard, I'd see her doing somersaults and cartwheels, following the lead of her two younger sisters.

Much to my amazement, Sarah kept pace with her younger siblings. Even though her muscles were loose and lank, she tried out every twirl and roll. She tried every unbalanced spin and awkward turn, confronting her disability with grit and boldness.

On her next birthday, we took Sarah and her sisters to a kid-friendly restaurant that offered an indoor playground that looked like a castle, a floor-to-ceiling gym decorated with colorful tunnels and turrets. While my husband and I ate pizza at a nearby table, Rachael and T. T. stayed close to the base of the gym, the two of them content to climb and twirl on ropes.

Sarah, however, leaped through the maze of shoots and ladders, climbing upward fearlessly, eventually disappearing from sight.

"Where is she?" I asked Don after we hadn't seen her for about fifteen minutes. He pointed to the very top of the gym, to a small turret marked with a yellow flag.

There I saw Sarah's face, smiling down at me as she looked through a small window. I knew it was Sarah because I could see the unmistakable sparkle of her pink-framed glasses.

"Sarah, that's too high. Come down...right now!" I shouted, as I looked toward the top of the gym while squinting.

I was scared she'd fall, scared that one of the other kids would bump into her, scared that she wouldn't be able to find her way back down.

Sarah didn't budge. She stayed right where she was. "Mom, it's nice up h-h-here…," she called down from her heavenward post. A good hour went by before we saw her again.

A few years passed. When Sarah was fourteen years old and her sisters were in their preteen years, our family took a summer vacation to the West Coast. On our way, we drove our mini-van through the mountains of Montana and Wyoming, stopping for roadside picnics and snapping photos of the buffalo and deer that dotted the rough terrain.

One afternoon, my husband steered our van toward the town of Ten Sleep, Wyoming. In the distance, I saw a stately mountain, beautiful to behold, yet intimidating in size. The mountain was covered with jagged rocks and lined with narrow roads that spiraled upward, like a toy slinky. As we drove closer to the base of the mountain, I looked out my front-seat window and saw a strange looking sign on the edge of the road. The background of the wordless sign was bright yellow, highlighted by the outline of a black truck, tipped upward on the side of a triangle. I'd never seen a sign like that in Minnesota.

"What does that sign mean?" I asked my husband.

"It's steep around here," he said.

From their back seats, my three daughters started giggling. "This should be good," T. T. said with a chortle. Now that the girls were older, they routinely teased me about my fear of high places.

"Don't worry Mom…we're in the Bighorn Mountains. The elevation is only 9,666 feet," Rachael said, as she scanned a map of Wyoming.

Sarah was sitting right behind me. "Mom…d-d-don't be s-s-scared," she said, patting me on the shoulder.

Our van began ascending as we circled around the lower

part of the mountain. There, towering pine trees were growing so close to the road that the kids started stretching out their arms to touch the branches as we drove by.

"Smells g-g-good...," Sarah said, as she breathed in the woodsy fragrance of the trees.

As we continued to circle upward, the tops of the pine trees got smaller and smaller. Now layers of clay-colored rock hemmed our van in on one side while a guardrail corralled us on the other. I kept my eyes fixed on the guardrail.

"I hope it's strong enough," I said. I started fantasizing about what would happen if we had a car accident. In my mind's eye, I saw our van toppling over the mountainside, rolling over and over against the stone and rock, tumbling into the trees below. *No one would find us...*, I told myself.

"Mom...l-l-look...," Sarah said, as she pointed to an eagle soaring above. Our car swirled around a narrow ridge, our tires just inches from the guardrail.

"I can't look....I can't," I squealed. I buried my head in my hands. I braced my feet on the dashboard. I felt queasy. My family just laughed.

Sarah leaned over the front seat. She pulled my hands away from my eyes.

"M-m-mm-mom...f-f-f-face y-y-your f-f-f-fears," she stuttered with firmness. She gently turned my face toward the window.

I took a deep breath. "Okay...okay," I said.

Though our van was now on an incline, slanting upward like a plane taking off from a runway, I opened my eyes. "I can do this...," I whispered.

A strange calmness came over me. Now that we were approaching the top of the mountain, the view was utterly spectacular. I could see for miles—valleys scooped out of rocks, blue rivers that looked like glittering party stream-ers, a salmon-colored sky that melted into the surrounding orange-clay hills. I couldn't find the words to describe the wonder of that moment. I could only imagine God looking down from heaven. *This is what he sees,* I thought.

Something wonderful was happening. I was doing what Sarah had done her whole life. I was confronting my handi-cap—my fear—by opposing it. I was taking a risk, facing my disability with boldness and grit.

I was looking at the world from a mountaintop. I was catching a glimpse of heaven from my car window, my castle turret in the sky. I was following Sarah's lead. I was jumping off the diving board of my insecurities, somersaulting into a pool of unprecedented beauty and joy. And it was fun.

"Mom…it's nice up…here," Sarah said.

"It is," I whispered.

Although four years have passed since that summer pil-grimage, the lessons that Sarah taught me on that mountain have changed my life. My Down syndrome daughter has taught me that I can't run away from my fears.

Just a few weeks back, it became clear that I had achieved victory over my fear of heights. On that sunny summer af-ternoon, I stood in the main-floor lobby of the Radisson, a high-rise hotel in downtown St. Paul. I had come to meet my publisher; he and two of his associates were in town for a conference.

"Let's meet for lunch at the Radisson. There's a nice res-taurant on the twentieth floor," my publisher had suggested.

Now I stood in the beautifully furnished atrium dressed in black pumps, a crisp white shirt, and pinstriped pants. I made my way to an elevator; it was completely enclosed with clear glass.

I can't do this...I can't, I told myself, as I frantically searched for a stairway. I shook my head in dismay. *This is ridiculous. I'm dressed up. I can't climb twenty flights of stairs,* I told myself.

I drew near to the glass elevator and pressed a black button that was trimmed with an upward arrow. I heard a "ding." I got in. The doors closed with a whoosh.

As the glass elevator ascended upward, I closed my eyes tightly. Then, as clear as could be, I heard Sarah's comforting voice ringing out from my memory.

"M-m-mom...f-f-face y-your f-f-f-fears...." The elevator climbed higher and higher. I opened my eyes.

I looked through the glass that hemmed me in. I could see a plane taking off from the airport and a barge floating on the gleaming blue waters of the Mississippi. I could see the sun reflecting off the windows of the surrounding sky-scrapers.

Sarah's Down syndrome face appeared in my mind's eye; her sweet slanted eyes, her sacred smile, sparkling. I kept my eyes open all the way up to the twentieth floor. As I stepped out of the elevator, my publisher and his associates greeted me with handshakes and warm hellos. They guided me to a table set with beautiful white linens and a vase of fresh flowers.

"It's nice up here," I told my publisher.

As the waitress began pouring lemon-scented water into our crystal glasses, I knew I was a changed woman. I was opposing my handicap. Because of Sarah, I was facing my fear.

Ponderings

fear, fer: a painful emotion, excited by expectation of evil or the apprehension of impending danger; anxiety. (New Webster Encyclopedic Dictionary of the English Language.)

What do you fear? Are you fearful about getting cancer or growing old…or losing your job? Do you anticipate that a disaster will touch you or your family?

Maybe you are haunted by a fearful childhood memory. Perhaps an experience from your past has left you feeling handicapped as an adult. Are you paralyzed when you see certain people? Do certain places trigger painful images from your past?

Sarah has taught me that fear is a disability—a high mountain that everyone, at some point, must surmount. Though the rough terrain of fear is often lined with the jagged rocks of past experiences, it is well worth the climb.

God understands our secret apprehensions. He promises to give us strength to face the things we fear most, the courage to hike upward, ever closer to the mountaintop of his love.

Just listen to the words of comfort from Psalm 18: "He made my feet like the feet of a deer, / and set me secure on the heights" (v. 33).

There's so much beauty in life. Don't miss it. Look at your life the way God does. Stand on the mountaintop of your fear.

You might be surprised. The view is nice up there.

TWELVE

Cry When You Have To

M y father passed away during Holy Week, just a few months after Sarah was born. He died of a heart attack while watching my brother, Timmy, play in a college hockey game, a national championship game that was held in Lansing, Michigan.

On the morning after his passing, I gathered with my extended family at the home we had grown up in. As we sat around the kitchen table, most of now young adults in our early twenties, Timmy recalled Dad's final moments of life.

"He was sitting with mom in the stands…I had just scored a goal….I looked up at Dad and he gave me a thumbs-up," Timmy remembered.

My mother dabbed tears from her eyes as Timmy continued with his story. "The crowd started cheering….I skated toward the bleachers….I looked up and Dad was leaning on Mom," Timmy said. My mother nodded. "He was gone…," she said softly.

At the funeral, my family sat together, holding hands as hopeful hymns were sung and beautiful passages were shared. While my husband and brothers and in-laws served as pallbearers, Annie sat on one side of me, rocking baby Sarah in her arms. On the other side, my sister Julie cradeled her newborn, Patrick John. She and her young husband had given birth to Patrick John just a few hours after Dad's death. They had named him after my father. Now as Patrick John's soft coos and cries filled the church, the priest began reading from the Book of Ecclesiastes: "There is an appointed time for everything, and a time for every affair under the heavens....A time to be born and a time to die...a time to mourn and a time to dance..." (see 3:1–4). As a family, we got through the service, resting in the unspeakable comfort of one another's presence.

In the weeks and months that followed, my family got together often at the old homestead for Sunday barbecues, birthday parties, and other family celebrations. Often, as we gathered around the kitchen table, we would share our favorite memories of Dad: "Remember the Sullivan Olympiad.... Don't forget all those times he made us polish our shoes. ...What about the rations on cookies?"

We laughed when it was right. We cried when we needed to. In time, our tears faded. In time, we adjusted to the loss of our father. In time, our precious memories of Dad overshadowed the heartache of his passing.

Though Dad's death happened during the same year that Sarah was born, both experiences taught me that the season of sorrow was never meant to last.

I sat in our mini-van, outside of the main entry of the high school, waiting for Sarah to finish up her school day. The afternoon bell rang loudly, vibrating through the parking lot for several noisy seconds. Soon the surrounding sidewalks and parking lots were filled with rambunctious teenage students, all of them talking, laughing, and roughhousing as they made their way to nearby cars and houses. In the midst of the masses, Sarah walked to our van, accompanied by her special-education teacher.

"Sarah had a hard day, " her teacher replied. I looked at my seventeen-year-old daughter. Wearing blue jeans and a sweatshirt. Her usual smile was gone.

"Sarah? Are you okay?" I asked. She said nothing.

A few days earlier, one of Sarah's classmates, a teen named Josh had passed away. I didn't know much about Josh except that he was severely disabled. I had often seen Josh when I visited Sarah's classroom for special programs and events. Though Josh was in a wheelchair, unable to walk or talk or focus his eyes, Sarah was always by his side.

Sometimes when I would drive Sarah home from school, she would talk about her school day, highlighting the experiences she had shared with her multiply handicapped friend.

"I ate l-l-lunch w-w-w-with Josh....I g-got-t to p-p-push Josh's w-w-wheelchair....I...I...I...h-helped...Josh throw a b-b-ball during g-g-gym," Sarah would tell me.

At the high school, Sarah and Josh were well known and respected by teachers and students alike. Each morning, Sarah would push Josh's wheelchair through the main floor hallways, the two of them delivering newspapers to nearby classrooms. They had developed an efficient delivery system.

"Josh h-h-holds...the...the...newspapers on h-h-his lap," Sarah would report.

But now Josh was gone and Sarah wore a look of dismay as she got into the front seat of our van. "I think she's grieving," Sarah's teacher replied.

I nodded. Since Josh's death, Sarah had been much quieter at home. She hadn't been eating much either. As I drove home, Sarah cried softly, tears streaming down her face. "Before he…he…he died, J-J-Josh g-gave me h-h-his 'valuable,'" Sarah said. She reached into her pocket and pulled out a small rubber ball trimmed with yellow strings. "I …played catch w-w-with Josh…he h-h-held this," she said.

I wasn't sure how to comfort her. Driving onward, I found myself thinking back on the early years of my daughter's life. When she was a newborn, she hardly ever cried. Maybe it was because she was so physically weak, her tiny heart in need of major repair. Or maybe it had something to do with her many mental limitations and the unpredictable quality of her Down syndrome.

"She won't develop at a normal pace…she may not know when to cry…we can't foresee what she will do," the doctors had said. Whatever the reason, I rarely saw tears fall from my daughter's eyes.

After Sarah's heart surgery, as she began learning to walk and talk, her smile was perpetual. I kept thinking that she would eventually communicate other emotions like sadness and sorrow.

When she would fall and skin her knee, she would whimper for just a moment, only long enough to catch my attention. "Mom…I…I…I…love you," she would whisper; at once forgetting her pain as I taped a Band-Aid to her scraped leg. When her younger sisters would have temper tantrums, Sarah would simply watch them throw toys across the room and listen to them wail loudly. "Be happy…be done," she would say as she walked out of the room holding her hands over her ears.

In those early years, Sarah was always coming up with new ways to share her irreprisible joy. I began remembering a spring morning when Sarah was about eight. A young mother, I had been taking care of Sarah and her two younger sisters for weeks; all three of them had gotten the chicken pox at the same time. Though the kids were on the mend, their faces were still dotted with the telltale pox.

"I've got cabin fever," I told Sarah one morning, as I looked out the kitchen window, wishing that I could take a long walk in the warm spring air.

"Momm...let's have...a-a-a...p-p-party," Sarah suggested.

With that, Sarah opened the kitchen cabinets and pulled out four mismatched plates, counting out one for me, one for herself, and two for her younger sisters. After stashing a few snacks into a paper bag, she made her way to the backyard and began setting our picnic table, trimming each unmatched plate with a slice of bologna, a handful of raisins, and a left over lollipop from Halloween.

That bright spring morning, as I sat with my little girls at the picnic table, Sarah put on a show for us. She sang the theme song from *The Brady Bunch*. Rachael and T. T. started dancing with Sarah, the three of them waving branches, their laughter echoing through the yard.

The first sunlight of the season felt warm and healing. Sarah's banquet, so lovingly prepared, was lifting my spirit.

"Sarah...this is great bologna," I said, chuckling as I chewed on my slice of meat.

"Mom...be d-d-done...n-n-no more s-s-sad," Sarah said, as she handed me a lollipop.

By the time Sarah was in the fourth grade, I'd gotten used to her constant optimism, each day it shone from her face like an angelic aura.

Then, on Sarah's twelfth birthday, I began realizing that Sarah was capable of feeling much more than mirth. That evening, my sister Annie came over to celebrate Sarah's special day. Now a newlywed, Annie's husband was away on a short business trip. Don was also away at a two-day teaching seminar. It was an "all-girls'" party.

Our kitchen was decorated with pink balloons and paper plates. T. T., Rachael, and Sarah crowded around Annie as she pulled three gifts from a bag. Rachael got a teddy bear. T. T. received a Raggedy Ann doll. On Sarah's birthday, Aunt Annie always gave each of the girls something special.

"And now…for the birthday girl," Annie announced as she waved a small gift she had wrapped in pink flowered paper.

Sarah opened the present. It was a Shirley Temple video, one that Annie and I had often watched in our youth.

"*The Little Princess*…I remember that movie," I shouted to Annie. It was a timeless movie classic about a child named Sarah, a wartime story about a little girl's painful separation from her "soldier-dad."

Annie knelt down next to Sarah, their eyes locking. "It's a sad movie. You might cry, but that's okay," Annie told my Down syndrome daughter.

Sarah was elated. "Oh, Annie…I-I…love it," she said, smiling as she hugged my sister tightly.

Later that night, after Annie left, I let the girls watch the video in our family room. While I cleaned up birthday dishes in our adjacent kitchen, I could hear the girls laughing as young Shirley Temple performed her usual song and dance routines.

Toward the end of the movie, a sad scene flashed across the television screen, one I had seen time and time again. I sat down on the couch, next to Sarah. I saw a wounded soldier, sitting in a wheelchair, bandages wrapped around his head. The battered warrior was in a hospital ward, repeating the name of his daughter, over and over again: "SARAH...SARAH...SARAH...."

My Down syndrome daughter turned her glance my way, tears streaming down her face. Real tears. Soon, her eyeglasses misted over.

"Sarah, are you okay?" I asked.

T. T. and Rachael drew near to their sister. "Mommy, Sarah is crying. What do we do?" they cried out as they comforted their Down syndrome sister with hugs. Like me, they had never seen this side of Sarah.

"The movie isn't real," I told my daughter, patting her on the back. She was inconsolable. I turned the movie off.

A few minutes later, I helped Sarah into bed. Just before she fell asleep, she dried her eyes and whispered, "Mom...I-I'm done."

I looked at her curiously. "You're done with what?" I asked.

Her smile was so wide that her eyes looked like little lines. "I'm done crying."

The next night, Sarah tried watching the Shirley Temple movie again. She sat close to my side. Just before the heart-wrenching hospital scene began, I jumped up to turn the TV off.

"M-M-Mom...it's...it's...it's...n-n-not real," Sarah told me. She quickly flicked the video button back on. She watched the movie until it ended with an unexpected finale, a tender father-daughter reunion. "See Mom...it's okay," she said.

But now, a few years had passed and Sarah was a teenager. She was growing up, experiencing real life, real relationships, real losses. Josh's death wasn't a movie. I couldn't turn off the video. I couldn't tell her "it's not real." That afternoon, as I drove Sarah home from high school, I just let her cry.

In the weeks and months that followed Josh's death,

Sarah dealt with her grief by carrying Josh's favorite "valu-able" in her pocket. She took the little rubber ball with her everywhere—to school, to church, to the store. Whenever she thought about Josh, she would take the ball from her pocket and look at it. Then, she would let her tears have reign. "Okay…I'm d-d-done," she would say after a few moments, her tears melting into a warm smile.

Sarah's grief was like wind. It blew into her soul when-ever it wanted to, stirring up memories and emotions, rus-tling up tears. Then it passed.

One Sunday morning while I attended morning Mass with Don and the kids. Sarah sat next to me, clutching Josh's "valuable" in her hands. Sunlight streamed down from the stained-glass windows above the altar, a colorful prism of light filling the church.

"M-m-mom, I…I…I-loved Josh," Sarah whispered.

I closed my eyes. I started to think about the times in my life when I too had experienced the kind of grief that Sarah was going through. I rewound my thoughts backward in time. Though my father had died the same year Sarah was born, Sarah's birth and diagnosis had demanded much more of me, at least emotionally.

Images of Sarah's life surfaced in my mind's eye, like a photo album brimming with pictures. I had known true sorrow at Sarah's birth. During her first days, the realities of her diagnosis seemed too much to bear. Like all first-time mothers, I had dreamed of giving birth to a child without impairment or limitation. Back then, I had gone through a period of grieving the loss of a child I had imagined.

I'll never be happy again, I had told myself a week after Sarah was born.

Then, there was Sarah's first day of school. On that September morning, I had dropped her off at a classroom labeled: Special Education. When I looked around the room, I saw that all her little classmates were handicapped, wheelchairs and medical equipment lining the walls of the room. Though I knew that Sarah's teachers and aides would give my daughter the extra care she needed, the inner ache I felt caught me off guard.

"Have a good day," I told Sarah, trying to conceal my sadness as I kissed my daughter good-bye. As I made my way out of the school, I passed a classroom labeled: Second Grade. The door of the room was open and I noticed children, twenty or so, standing beside their desks, reciting the Pledge of Allegiance.

"This is hard," I whispered to myself.

Throughout Sarah's growing-up years, I had been surprised by grief at the most inconvenient times. I remembered one Christmas when I attended Sarah's seventh-grade program. That year, Sarah's special-education class was performing with the regular junior-high-school choir. While I sat in a crowded gym, packed with proud parents, I watched as my Down syndrome daughter took her place on the risers, amid all the other "normal" preteen students.

When the choir began singing "Jingle Bells," a wave of emotion swept over me. My eyes welled up. In the darkness of the gym, Sarah stood out from all the other children, her smile, her low-toned facial muscles highlighted by the stage lights above. It was strange. There was hurt in my heart, but at the same time, I was thanking God, even praising God, that she was my daughter.

She is so beautiful, I thought.

Now, as I sat with my daughter in church, memories of Sarah's early years began to fade.

"Sarah, it's good you loved Josh," I whispered. The Mass continued as I put my arm around my daughter, grateful for her presence in my life.

Throughout the years, Sarah had loved Josh just as she had loved me, unconditionally. In my journey of mothering her, she had been there for me, guiding me through years of unfamiliar emotions and experiences.

Sarah had taught me that feelings "just happen," that joy touches our lives at unexpected times just as sorrow comes and goes, on its own schedule, not ours. Because of Sarah, I had learned that heartaches don't last forever and that hurt usually turns into hope.

I had also discovered that the experience of grief is like watching a sad scene from an old video. When sorrow surprises us, appearing without warning on the television screen of our lives, we must take a moment to look at it. Just look. We must feel whatever it is that we need to feel. We can't turn the movie off. In time, the story will get better. Life will go on and happiness will return and the love we have shared with others will give us unimaginable strength. At just the right time, we'll find ourselves saying, "Okay, I'm done crying."

I looked up at the stained-glass windows above the altar, a mosaic of light now dancing through the church.

"Sarah, maybe Josh is looking down on you from heaven," I whispered to my daughter. Sarah placed the small ball in my hands.

"When we...we...g-g-get home, let's put it...it...away," she said softly.

"Are you sure?" I replied.

Sarah nodded. "Josh is-is in my h-h-heart," she said, her face shining with a wise, all-knowing smile.

I thought of my dad. I could feel his presence. Lines of sunlight radiated from Sarah's face. I wrapped my hand around the little rubber ball.

I was proud of my daughter. She had grieved well. Now, it was time to move on.

Ponderings

grieve, grief (grēf): pain of mind, arising from any cause; sorrow; sadness. (New Webster Encyclopedic Dictionary of the English Language.)

Everyone "feels" grief at one time or another. It's an inconvenient emotion; one that often arrives unexpectedly, interrupting our contented lives with heartaches and broken dreams.

When a loved one dies, when a friend betrays us, when a child is born with a disability, it's natural to ask, "WHY?" Life shouldn't be hard. Life shouldn't be sad. Life shouldn't hurt. But, at times, life is hard. And it is sad. And it does hurt.

Though we all go through "seasons of sorrow," we can rest assured that God will see us through. During Sarah's infancy, when I was grieving her diagnosis, I often turned to a comforting passage in the thirtieth chapter of the Psalms: " Weeping may linger for the night, but joy comes with the morning..." (v 5).

Isn't it good to know that grief wasn't meant to last? Just look at God's illustrative creation. Without fail, night turns to day. After a rainstorm, the sun eventually shines. At the close of a long and bitter winter, the first breezes of spring promise warmth and healing.

Are you in a season of sorrow? If you are, try following Sarah's proven "guide for grieving."

> *Cry when you have to. Feel what you feel. Carry the "valuable" of God's love in your pocket. Hold onto it, clutch it tightly. Take it with you, wherever you go.*
>
> *One day, when you least expect it, you might find yourself saying, "Okay, I'm all done crying."*

THIRTEEN

Dream Big

I still have the yellow-flowered dress I wore for my senior prom. It's a little snug on me, but I can't bear to throw it out. Every now and then, I take it from the back of my closet, and remember a sunny May morning in 1974.

At seventeen years of age, I clomped down the stairs that led to my grandmother Mema's sewing room. My face streaming with exaggerated teenage tears, I plopped my "prom gown" on her worktable.

"It looks awful," I wailed. Mema put on her bifocals; carefully examining the formal I had sewn. The hem was crooked. The waistline was puckering. Threads hung from uneven seams. Mema shook her head.

"All it needs is the loving touch," she said, as she held a tape measure to a mismatched sleeve.

For the rest of the day, Mema and I worked side by side at her sewing machine, her shoe tapping the foot pedal as a spool of thread whirred and a needle buzzed and stitched.

As Mema mended raveling seams, she reminisced about her past...the hard times of the Depression, losing the farm, the war. As I handed her pins, I nodded, but I had heard all the stories before. Preoccupied with the present, I began to chatter on and on about my date for the prom.

"I think he likes me more than I like him," I admitted.

Mema smiled. "Maybe the dress will scare him off," she joked. We laughed.

When at last the final seams of the formal were sewn, Mema held the dress up to my shoulders.

"Try it on," she said.

As I donned the refashioned gown, I danced my way past her sewing machine, my hand grazing the back of my hair like I was a fashion runway model. Mema looked hopeful, her brown eyes framed with wrinkles that looked like smiles.

Though my prom night was memorable, I can't seem to remember what color tux my date wore, or where we went to dinner, or even where the prom was held. What I do remember about my prom day was the special time that I had spent with Mema. We had been uniquely present to each other, bonded by a common history; our lives threaded together with stitches of love and understanding. She had given me the gift of a memory, one that would resurface years later when Sarah went to prom.

Sarah stood in front of the fireplace, dressed in a blue-chiffon gown trimmed with sequins; a gown that my mom and sisters had carefully altered and pressed.

At eighteen years of age, Sarah's soft chestnut-brown hair was curled into waves. She looked so grown up, wearing a string of pearls—a gift from my sister Peggy. On her head, was a crown of flowers, a head wreath that Annie had sent special delivery from her new home in Michigan. "To Princess Sarah," Annie had written.

A young man named Chris linked his arm with Sarah's. Just a couple years older than my daughter, Chris grinned, his slanted eyes, filled with kindness. Looking handsome and debonair, he was dressed in a navy suit and a silvery tie.

It was a Saturday night in May, "Prom Night," the eve before Mother's Day. While Chris began telling Sarah about his new job at the grocery store, I stood with my friend Joanne, both of us focusing our cameras.

"Smile...say cheese," I said, as we began snapping pictures.

Joanne and I had been friends for eighteen years. Our kids, Sarah and Chris, were born two years apart, both of them diagnosed with the same disability.

"We've been through a lot," I told Joanne.

My friend nodded, her jewel-green eyes glimmering with wisdom. With her short hair styled fashionably around her forehead, her face shone with a glint of youth, even though she was in her early fifties.

"We have," she said, her words punctuated with light-hearted laughter. While the two of us kept taking photos, our cameras clicking and flashing, I started remembering the series of events that had led me to Joanne, just a few weeks after Sarah's birth.

In my mind's eye, I saw myself as a young mother. It was a frigid winter day, the snow falling softly. I was driving home from Children's Hospital with two-month-old Sarah sleeping by my side, in a car seat.

"Everything will be okay," I whispered, trying to reassure myself. I took a deep breath and sighed. Two hours earlier, I had taken Sarah to an appointment with a pediatric cardiologist.

"Your daughter has two holes in her heart and a valve

that needs to be reconstructed. We'll schedule the surgery for spring," the doctor had said.

His words cut like a freshly sharpened blade. I was just beginning to accept Sarah's many mental limitations. Now, I was being told that my baby had serious physical impairments as well. To make matters worse, in three weeks, my maternity leave would be over. I had promised my principal that I would finish out the remaining months of the school year, working as a part-time teacher, during the morning hours. I needed to find day care for my child.

"Maybe I should forget my job." Yet, I couldn't do that. With Sarah's medical bills mounting, our family needed the money.

Who will care for a mentally and physically handicapped child? I thought, as I turned into our driveway. I couldn't imagine anyone who would accept Sarah just as she was, a very "unnormal" baby; frail and fragile with weaknesses too many to count.

The next day, I mustered up enough energy to visit several daycare homes in our area. I took Sarah with me to every house, holding her in my arms as I chatted with potential providers.

"My daughter is a special child," I told each caregiver, as I explained what Down syndrome was. Though most of the child-care workers were kind, I got the feeling that they felt sorry for me. "How are you handling this?" they asked. One child-care worker wouldn't even hold Sarah. She just tilted her head to one side, looking at my baby with pity. That was the last thing Sarah or I needed—pity.

After a week of interviews, I was discouraged. Then one afternoon, as I laid Sarah down for a nap, I knelt beside her crib. "God, please lead me to someone," I prayed.

A few days later, the phone rang. "Nancy, I'm a nurse at St. Joseph's Hospital. My name is Joanne," the caller explained. Her voice was warm and reassuring. I immediately felt comfortable sharing my story.

"My baby was born at St. Joe's…just a few weeks ago," I told the caller.

Joanne listened as I rambled on about my Down syndrome child even though she had already heard about Sarah's birth from some other nurses she worked with.

"We have something in common," Joanne said when at last there was a break in the conversation. "I have a two-year-old son. He has Down syndrome, too," she said.

With that, Joanne invited me over for coffee, giving me directions to her home. "Come tomorrow, I don't live too far from you," she said.

The next morning I drove about twelve blocks to Joanne's home, an old Victorian house with a wraparound porch. Swaddling Sarah in a warm blanket, Joanne greeted me at the door, the snow falling all around us. As I stepped inside, I felt a rush of warm air blowing from the antique radiator in her living room. Joanne took Sarah into her arms.

"Oh…, she's so lovely," Joanne said, tenderly kissing my daughter's forehead.

I looked at the family pictures that hung on her living room wall. "Are these all your children?" I asked as I pointed to a framed photo of four little boys. Joanne nodded. "We're a good Catholic family," she said, chuckling.

I guessed that Joanne was a few years older than myself. With her hair cut into a cute pixie, she wore jeans and a T-shirt, and her eyes brimmed with warmth and depth.

"Come, I want you to meet Christopher," Joanne said.

With Sarah still in her arms, Joanne led me to the kitchen

where a little boy with almond shaped eyes was sitting cross-legged in front of a pantry closet. He was busy building a tower out of cereal boxes and crumbling saltine crackers all over the floor.

"Chris, this is Sarah," Joanne said, as she knelt down beside her son, unwrapping Sarah's blanket.

Chris brushed his hand over Sarah's face. "Tharah... beautiful," the little boy said, his voice endeared with a lisp.

Joanne looked up at me. "Nancy, you are beginning a beautiful adventure. Along the way, Sarah will teach you many things," she said.

I felt like I had known Joanne all my life. Though we had just met, she seemed more like family. We were connected, our lives immediately bonded by these two very special children. She was an experienced mother. I wanted to learn from her. I wanted to hear her stories.

"Joanne, I need to return to work. I wish I could find someone like you to watch Sarah. Do you know of anyone?" I asked. It was just a fleeting thought, spoken aloud.

"My mornings are free. When do you want me to start?" she said, smiling.

For the next few months, Joanne took care of Sarah, each morning from 7:30 to 12:30. Every afternoon, when I picked Sarah up, Joanne always had a cup of coffee waiting for me.

Often the two of us would sit on the living room couch, chatting while Chris played with Sarah. Even though my baby daughter could only lie on a blanket, her medical condition worsening with each day, Chris seemed to sense that she needed extra love and attention. He would pat her back. He would sing to her.

"Tharah...beautiful," he would say. Chris was Sarah's first true friend.

The weeks passed and my friendship with Joanne soon became a "lifeline" of strength and hope. Often, I would find myself asking her questions: "Where does Chris go to school? Does he have a speech therapist? How do your other children handle his disability?"

She always had a hopeful answer for me. "There is so much out there for our kids," Joanne said, as she talked about schools and community programs in the area. "Chris has made our family stronger. My children don't take his disability too seriously. They just accept him as he is," Joanne said.

During those afternoon conversations with Joanne, I started thinking about Sarah's disability in a whole new way. Instead of focusing on her numerous limitations, I began dreaming new dreams.

Maybe Sarah will *walk and talk and sing,* I told myself. It felt so good to have a different perspective. *Maybe we will have other children...maybe everything will be okay.*

The winter months soon turned to spring and the date of Sarah's impending heart surgery drew near. One afternoon in the month of May, just a couple days before Sarah's operation, Joanne and I sat at the picnic table in her back yard.

As I rocked Sarah in my arms, I noticed that my daughter's tiny hands were tinged with blue, a symptom that validated the grimness of her condition. I began preparing myself for the risky surgery that lay ahead. The words of Sarah's cardiologist began echoing through my mind: "It will be a long operation...after the procedure, your daughter will be in intensive care...she will be hooked up to monitors and breathing machines."

I was scared. "Joanne, I don't know if I can do this," I told my friend.

With gentleness, Joanne leaned over and took my baby into her arms. She held Sarah close to her heart and closed her eyes. "Nancy, God is good...everything will turn out okay," she said softly.

Now, eighteen years later, as Joanne and I snapped pictures of our grown-up kids, I knew that my friend had been right. Everything had turned out okay.

I smiled as Chris began telling Sarah about his "bagging" job at the grocery store. "I never, ever put bread in the bothum of the bag," Chris exclaimed, waving his palms for effect.

"I...m-m-m-make...m-my own greeting c-cards," Sarah replied, as she straightened her crown of flowers. "S-s-someday...I want to sell them...in...in a store," she added.

Joanne and I turned to each other, our eyes locking. Our children's childhood was coming to an end as another part of our mothering journey was just beginning.

"Joanne, they have their whole lives ahead of them," I said.

My friend nodded. "The adventure continues," Joanne replied.

A few minutes later, Joanne and I drove the kids to the high school and escorted them to a cafeteria decorated with beautifully set tables and glowing candles.

Just before the prom celebration began, Sarah and Chris lined up with all the other exquisitely dressed teen couples.

"And now for the Grand March," a teacher announced from a loudspeaker. When their names were called, Sarah and Chris began walking arm-in-arm down a long aisle lined with proud parents. From all parts of the room, cameras began flashing, lighting up the cafeteria like a press conference.

Oh, they look so precious...look at his smile...she looks

like a princess," came the happy whispers from the other parents.

After the Grand March, the band started playing "old-ies" from the 50s, 60s, and 70s. Joanne and I tried to blend in with all the other adult chaperons, standing beside the food buffet as Sarah and Chris sat down at a table donned with fine china and a vase of fresh flowers.

Chris was a perfect gentleman to my daughter. He pulled out her chair so that she could sit down. "Tharah, would you like thumthing to drink? Do you like chicken? Would you like to danceth?"

Sarah couldn't stop smiling. "Why, yes...I...I...I...love dancing," she replied, as she took Chris's hand.

From the sidelines, Joanne and I started chuckling as Chris taught Sarah how to do the "twist" and the Michael Jackson "moonwalk." When the band began playing "Blue Suede Shoes," Chris started imitating Elvis Presley, pivoting his shoes back and forth as he twirled Sarah.

"Who taught Chris how to dance so well?" I asked Joanne.

"His brothers," Joanne replied, as she rolled her eyes in fun.

At the end of the prom, Chris bowed to Sarah. "It was very fun," he told my daughter.

Sarah curtsied. "I...I...I...h-h-had ...a ... w-w-wonder-ful t-t-time," she said.

Later that night, as Sarah sat with our family at the kitchen table, all of us eating ice cream in our pajamas, she told us about her evening of enchantment.

"Chris taught me a...a...new d-d-dance...I ate chicken....I will...d-d-dream about this n-n-night forever," Sarah said.

From across the table, I looked at Sarah's face. After so many years, her Down syndrome features were starting to look like beauty marks. She had grown and changed into a young woman, everything about her appearance was lovely. How blessed I was. Because of her presence in my life, I too had known the beauty of growth and change.

Eighteen years earlier, Sarah had arrived in my life, a sacred surprise disguised as a handicapped baby. How could I have known then that Sarah would slowly transform every part of me—my mind, my heart, my soul, my perspectives, my relationships, my hopes, my dreams, my faith.

If it wasn't for Sarah, I would've never learned to face my own disabilities, my deepest fears, my hidden insecurities, even my lack of trust. I would have never discovered that walking, talking, and singing are small miracles, worthy of praise.

I would have missed opportunities to dance in church, to sell free lemonade, or to celebrate life with a slice of bologna. I would've gone through the last eighteen years without truly appreciating the comfort of family, the encouragement of enduring friends, or the unfailing power of God's love and faithfulness.

"Sarah...it's good to dream," I told her.

"It...it...is," she replied with a yawn. Minutes later, she feel asleep at the table, a smile on her face.

It's been six months since that prom night. These days, as Sarah continues to dream about her future, taking art classes and learning calligraphy, I find myself dreaming too. I dream that one day Sarah will have her own in-home art studio and that she will make a living at selling her cards and prints and necklaces. I dream that she will always have friends like Chris in her life, friends that look past her disabilities, friends that affirm her value and worth, friends that recognize how beautiful she really is.

I dream that when I grow old, really old, all the furrows on my face will look like smiles and that my children and grandchildren will never grow tired of hearing my stories. I dream that those I love will always love me, despite my numerous handicaps. I dream. I dream. I dream.

At the end of my days, I hope that I will be just as wise as Sarah. I want to look back on my life with a peaceful smile on my face. I want to rest in the knowledge that mothering a child with handicaps was a beautiful adventure and that every challenge of my daughter's disability was ultimately followed by an unexpected blessing.

Has it been hard at times? Of course. Would I do it all again? Oh yes. Sarah has, and continues to be, my teacher, my cheerleader, my personal coach from heaven. Thank you, sweet Sarah. You've taught me well.

Now I know that true intelligence is relative. Life's most important lessons *are* learned in the classroom of the heart.

Ponderings

"We know that all things work together for good for those who love God, who are called according to his purpose" (Rom 8:28).

REFLECTION

Welcome to Holland

BY EMILY PERL KINGSLEY

I am often asked to describe the experience of raising a child with a disability—to try to help people who have not shared that unique experience to understand it, to imagine how it would feel. It's like this....

When you're going to have a baby, it's like planning a fabulous vacation trip—to Italy. You buy a bunch of guide books and make your wonderful plans. The Coliseum. The Michelangelo David. The gondolas in Venice. You may learn some handy phrases in Italian. It's all very exciting.

After months of eager anticipation, the day finally arrives. You pack your bags and off you go. Several hours later, the plane lands. The stewardess comes in and says, "Welcome to Holland."

"Holland?!?" you say. "What do you mean Holland?? I signed up for Italy! I'm supposed to be in Italy. All my life I've dreamed of going to Italy."

But there's been a change in the flight plan. They've landed in Holland and there you must stay.

The important thing is that they haven't taken you to a

horrible, disgusting, filthy place, full of pestilence, famine, and disease. It's just a different place.

So you must go out and buy new guide books. And you must learn a whole new language. And you will meet a whole new group of people you would never have met.

It's just a different place. It's slower-paced than Italy, less flashy than Italy. But after you've been there for a while and you catch your breath, you look around…and you begin to notice that Holland has windmills…and Holland has tulips. Holland even has Rembrandts.

But everyone you know is busy coming and going from Italy…and they're all bragging about what a wonderful time they had there. And for the rest of your life, you will say "Yes, that's where I was supposed to go. That's what I had planned."

And the pain of that will never, ever, ever, ever go away …because the loss of that dream is a very, very significant loss.

But…if you spend your life mourning the fact that you didn't get to Italy, you may never be free to enjoy the very special, the very lovely things…about Holland.

Disability Resources

Books

Angel Behind the Rocking Chair: Stories of Hope in Unexpected Places by Pam Vredevelt. Published by Multnomah Press, 1999, <www .multnomahbooks.com>. In this inspirational book, the mother of a Down syndrome child shares true stories which offer reassurance to those who have struggled with God's design for their lives.

Count Us In: Growing Up With Down Syndrome by Jason Kingsley and Mitchell Levitz. Published by Harvest Books, 1994. Available at Barnes and Noble stores <www.bn.com> and at <www.amazon.com>. In this unique, groundbreaking volume, two young men with Down syndrome talk frankly about a full range of ideas, feelings, goals, and challenges. Entirely in their own words, the book covers such issues as having Down syndrome, friendship, marriage, children, school, politics, and their hopes and dreams for the future. While many books have been written about young people with Down syndrome, this book is written by the young men themselves.

Moments of Grace by Nancy Jo Sullivan. Published by Multnomah Press <www.multnomahbooks.com>. A collection of short, heartwarming stories. Many of the true life tales highlight the inspiring experiences of the handicapped and their families. These accounts reveal the subtle, deeply personal, life-changing activity of a large God who moves in divine partnership with his people—no matter how ordinary.

Sharing and Caring Hands: My Mondays With Mary Jo Copeland by Nancy Jo Sullivan. Published by Liguori Publications <www.liguori.org>. After spending ten Mondays at Sharing and Caring Hands, a Minneapolis-based ministry serving the poor and needy, Nancy Jo discovers new ways to live out her faith. Throughout the book, Sarah, Nancy Jo's disabled daughter, offers spiritual wisdom and insight.

Organizations and Resources

Joni and Friends: A nationally recognized Christian organization that provides support to the handicapped and their families. This program also provides churches with resources to support people affected by disabilities <www.joniandfriends.org>. JAF ministries, P.O. Box 3333, Agoura Hills, CA 91376. Phone: (818) 707-5664.

The National Catholic Partnership on Disability: Formerly the National Catholic Office for Persons with Disabilities, NCPD is committed to full inclusion of all disabled people in the church. The organization publishes a newsletter and resources <www.ncpd.org>.

The National Down Syndrome Society: Through leadership in education, advocacy and research, NDSS provides support for people with Down Syndrome and their families <www.ndss.org>.

The National Down Syndrome Congress: A national advocacy organization which provides leadership to persons with Down Syndrome <www.ndsccenter.org>.

Jeff Dunn Photography: Meaningful portraits for the handicapped and their families. Located on the border of Stillwater, Minnesota; <jdunn@pressenter.com>; (651) 439-5628; (715) 549-5222.

Rose Fitzgerald Kennedy Program: A sequential, developmental religious-education program for children and young adults with cognitive disabilities. The program includes 260 lesson plans, prayer services, and books for parents catechists. To order, contact: Sister Michelle Grgurich, VSC, Department for Persons With Disabilites, 135 First Ave., Pittsburgh, PA 15222; (412) 456-3119; www.diopitt.org/education/dpd.htm.